Playing the Soprano Recorder: Classroom Edition

Without Piano Accompaniments

For Church, School, Community, and the Private Studio

Playing the Soprano Recorder: Classroom Edition

Without Piano Accompaniments

For Church, School, Community, and the Private Studio

Lois Veenhoven Guderian

Published in partnership with
MENC: The National Association for Music Education
Frances S. Ponick, Executive Editor

Rowman & Littlefield Education
Lanham • New York • Toronto • Plymouth, UK

Published in partnership with
MENC: The National Association for Music Education

Published in the United States of America
by Rowman & Littlefield Education
A Division of Rowman & Littlefield Publishers, Inc.
A wholly owned subsidary of The Rowman & Littlefield Publishing Group, Inc.
4501 Forbes Boulevard, Suite 200, Lanham, Maryland 20706
www.rowmaneducation.com

Estover Road
Plymouth PL6 7PY
United Kingdom

British Library Cataloguing in Publication Information Available

Library of Congress Control Number: 2008928985

ISBN-13: 978-1-57886-830-8 (pbk. : alk. paper)
ISBN-10: 1-57886-830-0 (pbk. : alk. paper)

♾™ The paper used in this publication meets the minimum requirements of
American National Standard for Information Sciences—Permanence of Paper
for Printed Library Materials, ANSI/NISO Z39.48-1992.
Manufactured in the United States of America.

To my husband, Don, with many thanks for your encouragement and support in all of my musical endeavors and your work in helping to make this manuscript possible.

About the Author

Lois Veenhoven Guderian is a composer, choral conductor, music educator, performer, researcher, and clinician. Currently (2007) pursuing a PhD in Music Education at Northwestern University in Evanston, Illinois, Lois is the recipient of several awards from Northwestern including (2001) a three-year University/School of Music fellowship to pursue a PhD in Music Education, a Summer Music Educator Fellowship granted annually by Northwestern to ten music educators from the United States (2000), and the Emily Boettcher and J. Yule Bogue Scholarship for excellence in both musical and academic work (2003). Lois holds a Master in Music Education degree from Western Michigan University and Bachelor of Music degrees from Hope College in both Piano Performance and Vocal Music Education with a Major in Voice.

Lois has taught music, levels pre-K through university, in both public and private schools and is often a clinician/presenter on topics important to music education. She has designed curriculum for schools and organizations and specializes in writing sequential, discipline-based/interdisciplinary arts curriculum that incorporates music composition. She serves as a national adjudicator in music composition for the National Association for Music Education (MENC), as an adjudicator for the National Guild of Piano Teachers and for several music education organizations in Illinois. Lois is the Vice President and Education-Outreach Chair for the Chicago Composers Forum and formerly both Voice Chairman and Advocacy-Outreach Chairman for the Illinois State Music Teachers Association. In a special outreach program to the schools, "Link-UP – A Simple Melody" (2004), Lois worked as a liaison-teacher between the Chicago Public Schools and "arts partners," Weill Institute of Music at Carnegie Hall, Northwestern University, Ravinia, and Verizon Company. Lois is also very active in church music in a variety of capacities.

A choral director for many years of all age levels, in school, church, and the community, Lois specializes in beginning and building choral programs. Her groups have often been invited to be part of festivals or performances both in and outside of the Chicago area. Lois' choral compositions have been performed and recorded by several choirs including the Chicago Children's Choir; Coro Pro Musica Ensenada, Mexico; Barrington Children's Choir, Barrington, Illinois; and the Chicago District and Chamber Choirs of the New Apostolic Church. Lois often serves as a music teacher mentor or consultant for schools and organizations including the online *Chorus* mentorship for the MENC and as a music education reviewer for the nationally broadcast radio show *From the Top*.

A versatile composer and writer, Lois has written music for several publishing companies and accepts commissioned projects for commercial, educational and concert uses. She has authored texts in special areas of music education, and is a composer and writer for MENC. Her songs, piano pieces, instrumental and choral pieces and children's musicals are widely performed. Lois is published by co-publishers MENC and Rowman & Littlefield, Alfred Publishing Company (inclusion, *The Choral Warm-up Collection*), Transcontinental Music Publications, NAC of North America and LoVeeG Publishing.

Both an advocate and participant in music education research, Lois is interested in all issues surrounding music and arts education – especially those that deal with humankind's need for creative and spiritual expression. Her love for people and belief that all human beings have tremendous, musical and creative potential are the underlying forces that fuel her passion for music and arts education.

Table of Contents

Overview

Lessons

LESSON I   1

LESSON II

LESSON III

MORE SUPPLEMENTARY SOLOS   121

Foreword

Lois Guderian brings a wealth of experience as a teacher, musician, scholar, and writer to her materials for recorder performance. I was privileged to have her services as a teaching assistant at Northwestern University, and was able to observe her in each of those roles. Her intelligence and musicality are exceptional, as is her devotion to the musical education of people of all ages. I am not surprised, therefore, to have discovered how competently and expertly she has applied her abilities to instructional materials in an area in which she has deep interest and a wide background.

This project brings her strengths together in exemplary fashion, demonstrating how thoughtful pedagogical insights can be translated into practicable and engaging teaching-learning materials. The skills of performing, the workings of music notation, the use of diverse literature, the composing lessons, all add up to rich and satisfying experiences that will delight all who are lucky enough to study this fruit of her talents.

Teachers and students will find the instructions clear and concise and the arrangements solid and easily playable. The progression of learnings is carefully constructed, providing for both sequential development and a variety of challenges to keep things interesting. While theoretical learnings are accounted for they are related to and reinforced bountifully by their applications in music itself. The care with which the learnings are explained and expanded on insure clarity for both students and teachers, while allowing for room to explore related learnings that can be added as desired by those wishing to go off in a variety of directions. Structure and freedom are balanced nicely.

The musical examples represent an interesting, diverse collection of styles and types, adding to the attractiveness of the learning opportunities. Her accompaniments are appropriate and easily managed by teachers and students themselves who have some experience at the keyboard, adding to the enjoyment of class activities. The included CD offers an extra benefit in freeing the teacher from always having to accompany, thereby allowing full attention to what the students are doing. And the challenges of the "Creativity Corner" add an important dimension to those of performance, widening the sense students will receive of how the musical roles of composing and performing support each other.

Students engaged with these materials will both learn and enjoy; their musicality and their excitement about encountering the delights of being a performer will reinforce each other to the benefit of both. Each of the versions will serve its purpose admirably. Guderian has made an excellent contribution to the teaching and learning of recorder performance and to the musical education of those privileged to experience the wise, thoughtful guidance her material provides. I am gratified to have worked with and to know this admirable, enthusiastic music educator. And I envy those whose experiences in learning to perform will be as solidly based as she has enabled in this contribution she has made among so many others.

Bennett Reimer
John W. Beattie Professor of Music Education Emeritus
Northwestern University

Introduction

Learning to play the recorder and learning musical notation and concepts are introduced simultaneously in this course of study. *Playing the Soprano Recorder* is designed to develop playing skill, music reading, musicianship and creative thinking within the context of enjoyable, musical experience. It is an excellent foundation for instrumental and vocal music study that includes suggestions and opportunities for creative application of what the student learns. Teachers and students are encouraged to use the book as a framework and point of departure for their own creative ideas in teaching, learning and exploring music.

Playing the Soprano Recorder can be used in private instruction, in small and large group instruction, and in self-teaching. The age, ability and size of the group, as well as instruction time, will determine the amount of material learned in one session. Both in private and class study, students and teachers should proceed at their own pace as time allows. Each lesson contains sections on technique: one or two new musical concepts and terms; follow-up materials; pieces to practice, play, and perform; and opportunities to apply the newly learned concepts in creative ways (composition and other). All pieces in a given lesson reinforce the music and concepts learned in the lesson. There are two versions of *Playing the Soprano Recorder:* one for public school music education, private study and community and one for parochial school and church music education, private study and community. In the sacred version, one third of the pieces are arrangements of Christian hymns. In the secular version, all of the pieces are either original or arrangements of songs and music from historical music sources: American, ethnic, world, folk and Western classical.

When using this book, it is better to learn the materials in each lesson thoroughly before moving to the next lesson, as each new lesson builds on what has been learned in previous lessons. Students should be encouraged to practice at home. As is the case when learning to play any instrument, positive reinforcement, encouragement, and consistency in practicing are essential factors in student success. Student motivation to practice comes in large part not only from musical experience but from experiencing self-progress.

When sharing the book in music making with younger children, it is not necessary to read every word of instruction to them, such as how to hold the recorder, tonguing, etc. An experienced player can study and prepare to demonstrate these sections in advance of the time spent with the children. Showing, doing, and involving the children immediately with "hands-on" learning should by far outweigh verbal instruction. The written explanations are for older students, self-teaching and teacher reference. Most likely, younger children will take longer to cover the material than older children. A flexible approach is recommended. For additional pieces to play at each Lesson-level of difficulty there are two sections of additional recorder solos, "Supplementary Solos" found in Lesson XVIII and "More Supplementary Solos." Each time new notes on the recorder are learned, experiment and explore the possibilities for creating your own music. Add other instruments as well to your improvisations and compositions. Some suggestions are given at the end of each lesson. Add your own ideas to creating music from the first day of learning the fingering for pitches G, A and B.

One of the benefits of using this book is the possibility it opens for connections with other areas of learning. Many of the pieces have historical implications and can serve as a catalyst for or enrichment in interdisciplinary studies. Of these pieces, most include words for combined singing and recorder experiences. Other pieces have been arranged for instrumental ensemble and/or singers. All of the pieces and solos in the book have optional keyboard accompaniments arranged in various levels of difficulty to provide accompanying opportunities for many pianists. These are published in *Playing the Soprano Recorder Complete Edition(s): with Piano Accompaniment*. The materials in this book reinforce and "cross over" nicely into orchestra and band playing, choral singing, the private studio, Sunday school, regular school and private, personal enjoyment of music. The ensemble arrangements are appropriate for church services, school and community programs, recitals and other kinds of public performance.

Learning Tips

1. Reinforce your learning by teaching a friend how to hold, blow into, and play the recorder. Teach them the fingerings for notes (tones). To begin, face your friend and hold the recorder so they can see your fingers and model what you are doing. Then turn and face the same direction as your friend. Hold the recorder up with your left hand showing the left hand thumb placed underneath the recorder on the thumbhole. Make sure your friend understands right and left hand holding of the instrument. Face your friend again to show the fingerings needed for the notes (tones).

2. To gain ease in playing the recorder, learn the fingerings for the notes (tones) G, A and B and then play an echo game with a friend. Take turns making up short phrases of music that the other person copies and plays back. You can also play a game of musical questions and answers. One person creates and plays a musical phrase (question) and the other answers back with a musical phrase they create and play (answer). No notated music is necessary to play the games. At first, use only the fingerings for G, A, and B for the games. As you learn the fingerings for more notes (tones), add them to your bank of possible sounds to use in improvising and composing more musical phrases. During the game, try to keep the beat as steady as possible. Simply look at your friend just

before their turn to play so they are ready to play and to keep the beat going when you stop.

3. Sometimes, when learning new pieces and fingerings, it is very helpful to say the names of the notes aloud while playing the fingerings – without actually blowing into the recorder. It is also helpful to play the fingerings silently while counting the note values or rhythm of the piece aloud.

4. Make music flashcards (large or small size) for the note values such as quarter notes, half notes, and the music signs and symbols you learn for reading music. Share these with friends, a parent, a group, or your class by playing a game of recognition. On the back of each card, write the number of beats or name of the symbol so you can play the game alone as well. (After you name the sign or symbol, turn the flashcard over to check your answer.) Creating flashcards that picture the staff with one note to recognize can help in reinforcing music reading. You can also create flashcards with short phrases of music for friends to play. Staff paper is provided at the back of the book for creating your own music. Make several copies of the staff paper so you have many sheets for your creating and composing.

5. Counting and clapping the rhythm of a new piece before playing it often makes the piece easier to read, learn, and play.

6. Saying the note names of a piece aloud before playing it reinforces note reading on the staff.

7. When you have learned to play a piece with ease, play along with the piano accompaniment part on the practice and performance CD. This will help you to keep a steady beat in your playing, and it is enjoyable to play along with the added sound of the piano part.

8. Keep isopropyl (rubbing) alcohol and tissues on hand for cleaning the mouthpieces, or wipe the mouthpieces clean with an antibacterial cloth. You can also carefully wash the mouth piece with soap and water. Another part of the recorder that needs frequent cleaning is the inside. Many recorders are sold with cleaning sticks inside the case. Thread a small piece of cloth through the opening in a cleaning stick made for the recorder. Take the recorder apart – some have two pieces and others three. Slide the stick and cloth into the large hole of each piece and rub up and down to clean out the inside of the recorder and to absorb any moisture that the recorder might have built up from your practicing and playing.

9. Make your own music book by placing your written compositions in a binder. You can copy these for your friends and classmates to play as well as for your own playing enjoyment. When you write your music down in order to remember it or share it with others to play, it exists in a symbolic form referred to as "music notation." There are different kinds of music notation. The pieces in this book are notated in the Western music tradition. Many countries in the world use this same symbolic form for writing music. Try writing your compositions in Western notation and try creating your own system of notation as well. Ask your teacher, parents or friends for help if you have

questions about the process. Experiment with composing music for more than one recorder by adding voice and other instrument parts.

10. Each lesson in this book has several pieces to play that reinforce the new musical ideas, concepts, and fingerings introduced in the lesson. For more pieces that reinforce the same ideas and musical learnings, look in Lesson XVIII: Supplementary Solos. Still more pieces to play are found in the More Supplementary Solos section.

11. Move at your own pace through the materials in this book. Each lesson builds on what you have learned in earlier lessons by adding new things to learn about music. The new concepts are presented in a musical way in the new pieces in each lesson.

12. Many of the recorder pieces in this book are arranged songs. A song is music for the human voice. Create group music making experiences with your friends by singing and playing the pieces in this book that include words. Some pieces have more than one voice part, and others are for group or solo singing on one melody line. Other pieces have extra instrumental or recorder parts for group ensemble playing. You can compose additional instrument parts to add to the songs and pieces.

13. The Creative Corner section of each lesson gives you ideas for creating and composing you own music.

14. Everyone likes to learn how to play instruments, sing, and create music, and everyone can learn how to make music in these ways. Learning to play instruments and to sing on pitch and in parts require consistent effort, but the process can be very enjoyable. Each culture in the world has unique ways of making music,

singing, and instrument playing that have evolved over time. Today, we have many opportunities to learn the musical practices of our own culture and those of other cultures in school, at home, in our community, perhaps in private study, by listening to the radio, jamming with friends and through the internet we can connect with "musics" thousands of miles away. We are indeed rich in music and musical styles. Making, creating and listening to music are very special and beneficial activities that help us to learn and know things about ourselves and our world.

Playing the Soprano Recorder and the National Standards for Music Education

Playing the Soprano Recorder addresses all of the National Standards for Music Education in practical ways that can support music educators' efforts to meet individual state standards.

1. Singing, alone and with others, a varied repertoire of music

All of the pieces in the book that were originally songs have the words included for ensemble singing and playing. Because singing is included in a large way in this book, music educators have many opportunities to work on vocal technique as well. The arrangements are such that many of the songs can stand alone as possible contest or performance solos.

2. Performing on instruments, alone and with others, a varied repertoire of music

In addition to solo or unison soprano recorder playing, several of the pieces are arranged for optional two-, three-, and four-part soprano recorder. Some pieces include an optional alto recorder part, as well as Orff barred instruments, and strings. For some songs and pieces, parts can also be adapted for recorder consort or other instruments. Guitars, autoharps, and other classroom instruments are natural, musical additions to the arrangements. Piano parts are written in a variety of levels so children at varying levels of piano study can learn a piece and accompany the class. Due to the flexibility in adaptation and the addition of parts in varying levels of musicianship, the text is an excellent source for differentiated teaching and learning strategies in the general music classroom.

3. Improvising melodies, variations, and accompaniments

The Creative Corner sections feature opportunities and suggestions for improvisation. Teachers new to teaching improvisation and composition will find the text understandable, non-threatening and very "hands on" for both teachers and students. It can stimulate creative thinking and explorations in music, reinforce note reading, and help students develop tools for writing music in traditional and nontraditional music notation.

4. Composing and arranging music within specified guidelines

Creative work that directly relates to and reinforces lesson content is embedded into each Creative Corner as a way to nurture creative thinking in music and beginning music composition. The improvisation and composition activities can be completed in fewer than 30 minutes, partially completed with some carry over to another day, or be expanded for exploring and sharing creative work.

5. Reading and notating music

Music reading and notation are presented in a sequential, consistent, progressive, and logical way as part of each lesson. The lessons and Supplementary Solo sections reinforce note reading, give teachers and students a large variety of music to learn and perform, and provide advanced students a chance to work ahead or learn additional literature.

6. Listening to, analyzing, and describing music

The CD accompanying the book has recordings in multiple styles, both vocal and instrumental. Students have a sense of participation in a larger work when they have personally experienced the melody by playing it and, as a result, are usually able to pick it out as the main theme of a piece. Teachers can use the literature and concepts introduced in the book to augment other areas of music instruction and related listening experiences. Class discussions, written descriptions, comparisons, and group presentations based on the music presented in this book are all possible avenues of exploration.

7. Evaluating music and music performances

The pieces in this book are suitable for performance in conjunction with assemblies, programs, concerts, services, interdisciplinary and integrated collaborations. Rubrics, portfolios (recorded examples, etc.), and other means of assessment can serve students and teachers in the form of self, peer, and teacher evaluations. Recording solo and group performances as well as creative work in the classroom for playback and self-evaluation can be interesting and useful.

8. Understanding relationships between music, the other arts, and disciplines outside the arts

The possibilities for creating integrated, interdisciplinary and interrelated teaching and learning connections between the musical concepts and literature offered in the book and other disciplines are numerous. The discipline-based, sequentially organized format of the book facilitates interdisciplinary linkages as well as expansions and links to other areas within the discipline of music.

9. Understanding music in relation to history and culture

The music teacher can use the material in this book to link to lessons in history, social studies, art, literature, poetry, and drama, as well as to other music. Many of the songs stem from historic periods in American history (e.g., *Chester; Amazing Grace; Swing Low, Sweet Chariot / Nobody Knows the Trouble I've Seen; Battle Hymn of the Republic*), or from the Renaissance (*Greensleeves*). Some are from other countries (e.g., *Vive la Compagnie, Du Liegst Mir im Herzen, Hatikvah*). Possibilities for research, exploration, comparison, discovery, and performance offer rich learning opportunities. In addition, presenting choral, operatic, and instrumental versions of the music to the class, and ensuring ample opportunity for students' own singing, playing, and performing will expand and ensure students' understanding and enjoyment.

Fingering Charts

The following diagram will serve in learning the fingerings of notes for recorder playing throughout the text.

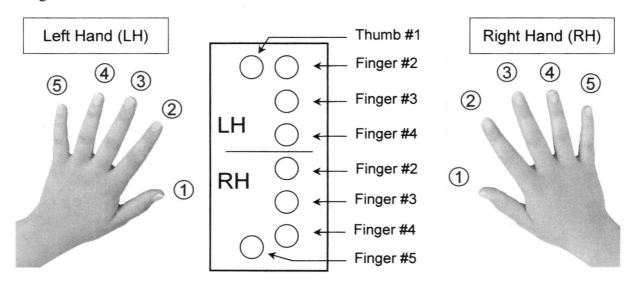

Understanding The Hole Coverings

- ○ - no cover
- ● - complete cover
- ◐ - approximately half covered
- ⊖ - left thumb covers a little more than half

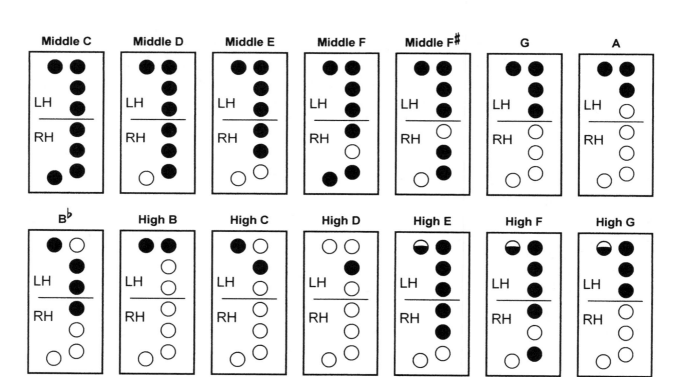

Playing the Soprano Recorder

Lessons

PLAYING THE SOPRANO RECORDER
A Soprano Recorder Music Method

LESSON I

TECHNIQUE AND FINGERING

Learning How to Hold the Recorder

All recorders, no matter the size, are held with two hands. The three holes closest to the face are played with the left hand. The left hand thumbhole is located underneath the recorder. The pinky of the left hand is not used. The right hand fingers cover the holes on the bottom half of the instrument with the pinky covering the last hole, to the right of the other holes. The right hand thumb is positioned underneath the recorder for support.

The following diagram will serve in learning the fingerings of notes for recorder playing throughout the text.

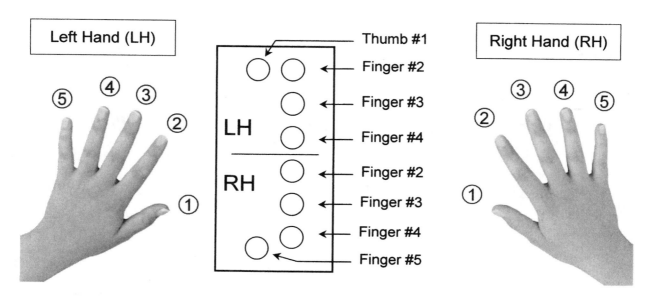

Understanding the Hole Coverings

○ - no cover

● - complete cover

◐ - approximately half covered

⊖ - left thumb covers a little more than half

Tonguing

Use your tongue to start and stop the notes when playing the recorder. This is called tonguing. Place the recorder mouthpiece between your lips (about ¼ inch of the mouthpiece). Pressing your lips together lightly, hold the recorder in place, making sure that the tip of the mouthpiece is not touching the tongue or teeth. With the recorder held between your lips, softly say the syllable "tah". In order to develop the correct technique for tonguing, try the following exercise: Breathe in and exhale a steady stream of air flow while saying the "tah" syllable several times without the recorder in your mouth. Repeat the process with the recorder placed between your lips.

Blowing

Breathing in and blowing gently into the recorder should be as consistent as possible. Try the following method:

1. Breathe in evenly through the mouth or nose.

2. Blow into the recorder with even and consistent exhaling of the breath. Too much air (over blowing) or too little air (running out of breath) will affect the pitch of the tone.

3. Breathe in and play the "tah" syllable for several seconds, or beats. Long held tones can be stopped by making the "d" sound with the tongue.

The First Three Notes

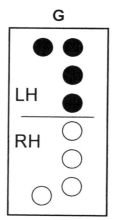
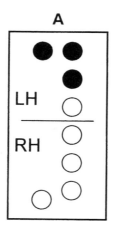
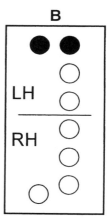

Find G, A, and B on the recorder. Be sure to cover the appropriate holes completely with the fleshy part of your fingertips. Breathe in and play "tah" for each new note. Stop the tone by making the "d" sound with the tongue.

MUSIC LESSON

Music Notes

Music notes are symbols for writing, reading and playing music. The shape of a music note is a flattened circle called a "note head." Most note heads have attached lines called stems. When the stem is attached to the right side of the note head the direction is up and when attached to the left side, the direction is down. Some note heads are colored in, and some are not. Music notes have duration or "value" of time which is measured in beats. The value of the note is how many beats or partial beats it receives in defined patterns. In many patterns used to notate music, the quarter note, as pictured below, receives one beat.

THE QUARTER NOTE ——————   —————— **RECEIVES ONE BEAT**

Clap the following quarter note exercise. Each note receives one clap of equal duration.

Exercise #1

Find the fingering for G on the recorder. Now play Exercise #1 using the fingering for G. Play the exercise again using the fingering for A, and then again using the fingering for B.

THE HALF NOTE ——————   —————— **RECEIVES TWO BEATS**

In music where the quarter note receives one beat, the half note receives two beats. Rhythm is the result of organizing beats and note values in time. Clap and play the rhythm of Exercise #2: First on G, then A, and finally B. Clap or tongue "tah" once for each note. Hold out the second beat of the half note. Count aloud while clapping, and silently while playing.

Exercise #2

Count:														
Clap:	1	1	1 - 2	1	1	1 - 2	1	1	1	1	1	1	1 - 2
Recorder:	tah	tah	tah - ah	tah	tah	tah - ah	tah	tah	tah	tah	tah	tah	tah - ah

Now try *First Piece*. Make sure your "finger pads" (the fleshy middle section of the last joint on the finger) are covering the correct holes on the recorder.

LESSON I PIECES

First Piece

Music by Lois Veenhoven Guderian

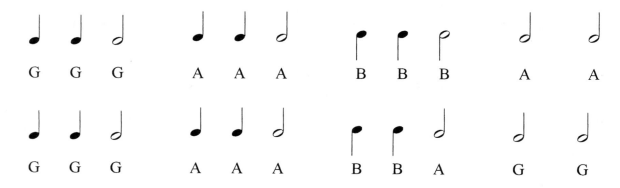

Clap the rhythm of *Now The Day Is Over*. Play the piece on your recorder.

Now the Day is Over

Words by Sabine Baring-Gould

Music by J. Barnaby (1869)
Arr. by Lois Veenhoven Guderian

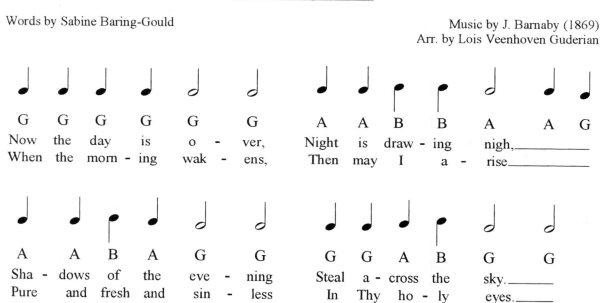

4

Clap the rhythm of *Prelude I.* Play the piece on your recorder.

Prelude I

Music by Lois Veenhoven Guderian

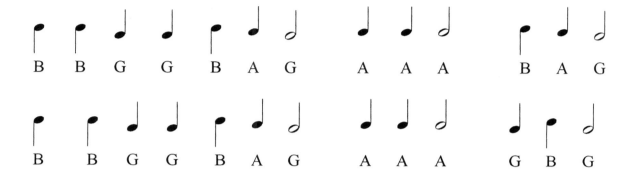

| B | B | G | G | B | A | G | A | A | A | B | A | G |

| B | B | G | G | B | A | G | A | A | A | G | B | G |

CREATIVE CORNER

1. Using the notes G, A, and B, compose your own piece.

2. Use only quarter notes (♩) and half notes (♩).

3. Make your piece as long or short as you would like it to be.

4. When your piece is finished, practice and play your piece.

5. Have a friend play your piece.

6. Give your piece a title.

7. Write as many pieces as you would like and have fun composing!

Example:

G   G   G   A   A   A   G   A   G   G

Composition:

THEORY AND TERMS FROM LESSON I

Quarter Notes (♩) — receive one beat.

Half Notes (♩) — receive two beats.

Rhythm — the result of organizing beats and note values in time.

ASSIGNMENT

1. Practice the tonguing and blowing technique in Exercise #1.

2. Practice the half note exercise in Exercise #2.

3. Practice **LESSON I PIECES**: *First Piece*, *Now the Day Is Over,* and *Prelude I* three times or more per day.

4. Learn and memorize the **THEORY AND TERMS** of **LESSON I**.

5. Complete the **CREATIVE CORNER** assignment.

6. Keep a record of how many minutes you practice each day.

M	TU	W	TH	F	SA	SU

LESSON II

TECHNIQUE AND FINGERING

Review the fingerings for G, A, and B, by practicing Exercise #3. In order to tongue clearly, be sure to say "tah" for each note.

Exercise #3

G   G   A   A   B   B   A   B   B   A   A   B   A   G   B   G   B   A   G

MUSIC LESSON

The Music Staff

Music notes are placed on a staff. The music staff has five lines and four spaces.

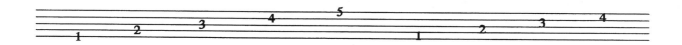

The middle of the note head is placed on a line or space.

Treble Clef (G Clef)

When the treble clef (G clef) sign is placed at the beginning of the staff, the second line is named G. (Notice how the treble clef circles around and ends just passing through the second line from the bottom of the staff). The music notes for soprano recorder are treble clef notes. The music notation for children and women singers, medium to high pitched instruments, the right hand part for all keyboard instruments and Orff instrument parts are also notated on a treble clef staff. You have already learned how to play the second line treble G on your recorder in Lesson I.

G Line, G notes

When placed on the second line of the treble clef staff, these quarter notes become G quarter notes.

A Space, A notes

When placed on the second space of the treble clef staff, these half notes become A half notes.

B Line, B notes

When placed on the third line of the treble clef staff, these quarter and half notes become B quarter and half notes.

Reading Music on the Staff

Music notes are placed on the staff in three ways:

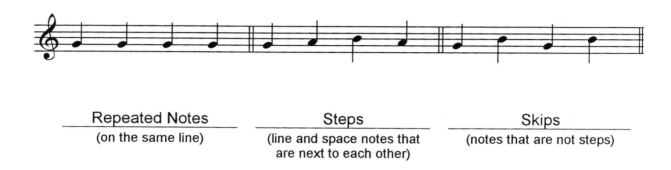

Repeated Notes	Steps	Skips
(on the same line)	(line and space notes that are next to each other)	(notes that are not steps)

Play the following piece comprised of many repeated notes: Be sure to tongue each note.

Piece of Repeat!

Play the following piece comprised of all steps.

Every Step Counts!

Play the following piece comprised mostly of skips.

Skipping with so Few!

Dotted Half Note

THE DOTTED HALF NOTE ——— 𝅗𝅥· ——— **RECEIVES THREE BEATS**

In music where the quarter note receives one beat, the dotted half note receives three beats. Clap the following rhythm pattern and then play the pattern using the fingering for G, then A, and then B.

Exercise #4

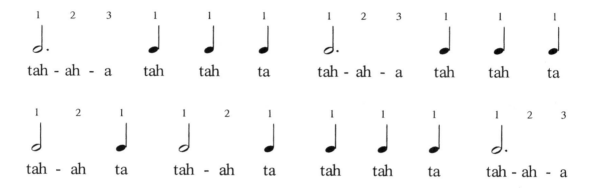

LESSON II PIECES

Stop and Look

Music by Lois Veenhoven Guderian

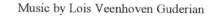

Waltz

Music by Lois Veenhoven Guderian

Breathe on Me Breath of God

Words by Edwin Hatch (1835-1889)

Music by Robert Jackson (1842-1914) (1878)
Arr. by Lois Veenhoven Guderian

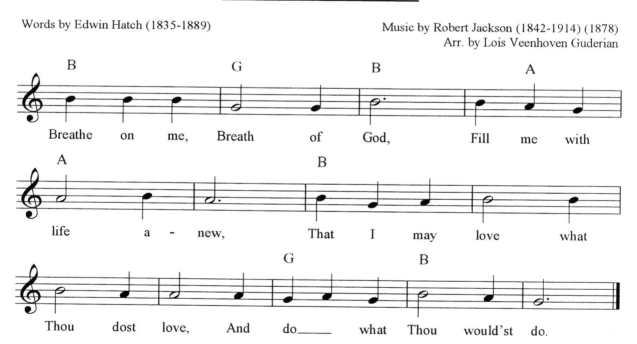

Faith of Our Fathers

Words by Frederick W. Faber

Music by H. F. Hemy
Arr. by Lois Veenhoven Guderian

CREATIVE CORNER

On the staff provided, write your composition from Lesson I.

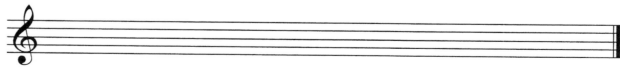

THEORY AND TERMS FROM LESSON II

Music Staff — has five lines and four spaces. Music notes are written on the staff.

Step — a space note followed by the very next line note, or a line note followed by the very next space note.

Repeated Notes — notes on the same line or space in succession.

Skip — any distance between two notes that is larger than a step, e.g., a line note to the next line note.

Treble Clef — also called G Clef. Establishes the second line of the staff as G, used in notating notes higher in pitch than Middle C.

Notation — (notating, to notate) the writing of music. Notes on the staff indicate pitch. Note values indicate rhythm.

Dotted Half Note (♩.) — receives three beats.

ASSIGNMENT

1. Practice Exercise #3 at least three times each day.

2. Study and practice all the examples in the section **Reading Music on the Staff** (on page 9).

3. Practice clapping the rhythm of Example #4 each day.

4. Practice **LESSON II PIECES**: *Stop and Look*, *Waltz*, *Breathe on Me Breath of God* and *Faith of Our Fathers* three times or more each day.

5. Complete the **CREATIVE CORNER** assignment.

6. Learn and memorize the **THEORY AND TERMS** of **LESSON II**.

7. Teach your favorite piece to a family member or friend.

8. Keep a record of how many minutes you practice each day.

M	TU	W	TH	F	SA	SU

LESSON III

TECHNIQUE AND FINGERING

Review the fingering and staff placement for G, A, and B by practicing Exercise #5.

Exercise #5

MUSIC LESSON

Time Signature

At the beginning of a piece of music, there are two numbers. These numbers are called the "time signature" (Examples: 4/4, 3/4, 2/4). The time signature determines the grouping of beats into measures. Measure bar lines separate the measures.

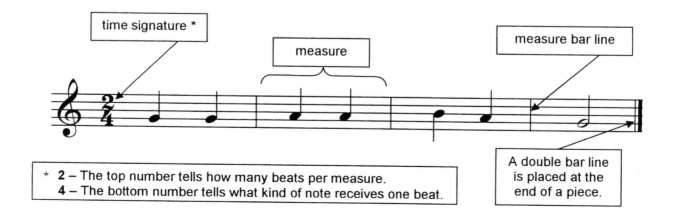

Read the following aloud for practice.

        2 – There are two beats per measure.

        4 – The quarter note receives one beat.

        3 – There are three beats per measure.

        4 – The quarter note receives one beat.

        4 – There are four beats per measure.

        4 – The quarter note receives one beat.

Whole Note

THE WHOLE NOTE ——— **O** ——— **RECEIVES FOUR BEATS**

In music where the quarter note receives one beat, the whole note receives four beats. Clap on the first beat of the whole note and hold your hands together while counting out the other three beats. All four beats must be at the same, steady speed. Clap and count several whole notes. Play several whole notes.

O

Count: 1 (– 2 – 3 – 4)

O

Play: Tah__ah__ah__ah__

Clap the rhythm in Exercise #6. Now play Exercise #6 on G, then A, and finally B. Clap or tongue "tah" one time for each note. Hold out the additional beats of the whole notes. Count aloud while clapping, and silently while playing.

Exercise #6

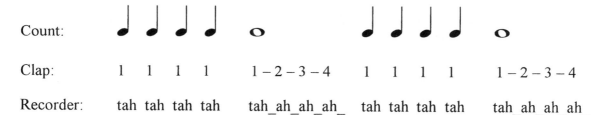

Count:	♩ ♩ ♩ ♩	𝅝	♩ ♩ ♩ ♩	𝅝
Clap:	1 1 1 1	1 – 2 – 3 – 4	1 1 1 1	1 – 2 – 3 – 4
Recorder:	tah tah tah tah	tah_ah_ah_ah_	tah tah tah tah	tah_ah_ah_ah_

LESSON III PIECES

Piece

Music by Lois Veenhoven Guderian

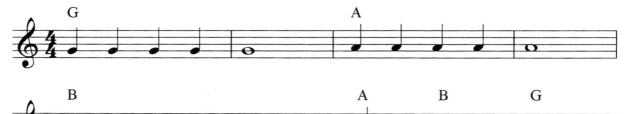

Almost a French Folk Song

Music by Lois Veenhoven Guderian

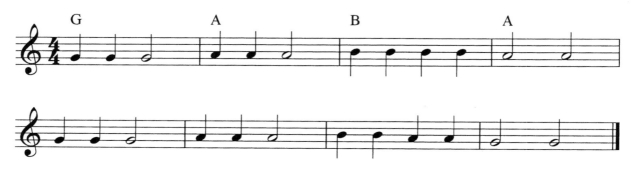

Praise God from Whom All Blessings Flow

Genevan Psalter
Arr. by Lois Veenhoven Guderian

Hot Air Balloon Waltz

Music by Lois Veenhoven Guderian

CREATIVE CORNER

Using the staff below, create your own piece (composition). To find ideas for your piece, explore sound possibilities by making up and playing rhythm and melody patterns on your recorder.

- Try creating and notating your composition in 2/4, 3/4, or 4/4 time signature.

- Use any combination of quarter, half, dotted half and whole notes (when possible).

- Use G, A and B notes or others you might have learned how to play.

- Make sure each measure has the same number of beats as found in the time signature.

- Use measure bar lines to separate the measures.

- Make your piece approximately four to eight measures long.

- Draw the double bar at the end of your composition.

THEORY AND TERMS FROM LESSON III

Tip for Writing Notes Correctly

On the staff, notes placed on the middle line and above have stems that go down, on the left side of the note head. Notes placed below the middle line have stems that go up, on the right side of the note head. G and A are <u>up stem</u> notes. B is a <u>down stem</u> note because it is on the middle line.

Time Signature — determines the grouping of beats into measures.

Measure — the music in between two bar lines.

Measure Bar Lines — separate the measures.

Double Bar — is placed at the end of a piece of music.

Whole Note (o) — receives four beats.

ASSIGNMENT

1. Practice Exercises #5 and #6 each day.

2. Learn and practice *Piece, Almost A French Folk Song, Praise God From Whom All Blessings Flow,* and *Hot Air Balloon Waltz* three times each day. Did you find any whole notes in these pieces?

3. Learn the new signs and symbols from **LESSON III**.

4. Complete the **CREATIVE CORNER** section.

5. Learn the **THEORY AND TERMS** from **LESSON III**.

6. Keep a chart of how much time you practice each day.

M	TU	W	TH	F	SA	SU

LESSON IV

TECHNIQUE AND FINGERING

<u>**Two New Notes – C and D**</u>

C   **D**

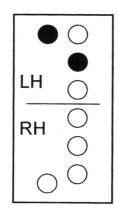 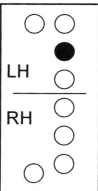

Practice Exercise #7 to learn the fingering for C and D.

<u>**Exercise #7**</u>

MUSIC LESSON

<u>**Eighth Note**</u>

THE EIGHTH NOTE ——— ♪ ——— **RECEIVES ½ OF A BEAT**

Two eighth notes beamed together () are equal to one quarter note. Therefore, in music where the quarter note receives one beat, two eighth notes are equal to one beat.

Eighth notes are faster than quarter notes. In order to play eighth notes on the recorder, tongue quickly by saying "teh." You will feel your tongue moving quickly to play the shorter value eighth notes. Practice Exercise #8 on each of the five notes you have learned. First, clap and count the exercise.

Exercise #8

Clap:

Count: 1 & 1 & 1 1   1 & 1 & 1 - 2   1 & 1 & 1 1   1 & 1 & 1 - 2

Recorder: teh teh teh teh tah tah teh teh teh teh tah_ ah_   teh teh teh teh tah tah teh teh teh teh tah_ ah_

LESSON IV PIECES

Little Bird

Music by Lois Veenhoven Guderian

Chester

Adapted from lyrics by William Billings

Music by William Billings (1778)
Arr. by Lois Veenhoven Guderian

When we are met with chal - len - ges and strife,   Prob - lems and wor - ries that would

drag   us   down.   We   fear them   not   we___   trust_____ in

God.   God   is   for   us,   Who can be a - gainst us? Praise him   e - ver   more.

From Brahms' First

Adapted from J. Brahms' Symphony no. 1 in C Minor
By Lois Veenhoven Guderian

Twenty-First-Century Minuet

Music by Lois Veenhoven Guderian

CREATIVE CORNER

Rhythm Sounds Composition

Compose a "rhythm sounds composition" using eighth notes and any of the other notes you have learned. Any object or "sound" can become an instrument. Use traditional and/or homemade rhythm instruments in your composition. Assign parts to your classmates. Practice and perform your piece in class. Example:

Write your composition here:

Homemade Instruments

Homemade Maracas

Take plastic eggs (the kind available before Easter) and fill with dried peas, beans or rice. Decorate with permanent colored markers, paints, or colored paper if desired.

Homemade Drum

Take empty oatmeal cartons or metal coffee cans and cover with colored paper. Use the lid as a drumhead, or stretch a piece of vinyl tightly over one end of the container, securing it with a rubber band. Play the drum by tapping the drumhead lightly with the fingers. Decorate the outside of the drum if desired.

Homemade Rhythm Sticks

Use unsharpened pencils (either end makes a good sound), chopsticks or plastic spoons.

THEORY AND TERMS FROM LESSON IV

Eighth Note (♪) — receives ½ beat.

Two Eighth Notes (♪♪) or (♫) — receive 1 beat.

ASSIGNMENT

1. Practice Exercise #7 with new notes C and D.

2. Practice Exercise #8 with eighth notes.

3. Practice the new pieces of **LESSON IV**: *Little Bird, Chester, From Brahms' First* and *Twenty-First-Century Minuet*.

4. Complete the **CREATIVE CORNER** section by composing a "rhythm sounds composition."

5. Learn the **THEORY AND TERMS** from **LESSON IV**.

6. Keep a chart of your practice time.

M	TU	W	TH	F	SA	SU

LESSON V

TECHNIQUE AND FINGERING

Review the fingering for notes C and D by practicing Exercise #9.

Exercise #9

MUSIC LESSON

Dynamics: Louds and Softs of Music

Composers show how loud or soft a section of music should be by writing signs and symbols in the music. Performers and music makers add expression to their music by adding louds and softs.

p is the sign for playing music softly. It is an abbreviation for the word *piano* in Italian. *Piano* means soft.

f is the sign for playing music loudly. It is an abbreviation for the word *forte* in Italian. *Forte* means loud.

Play Exercise #10 being careful to observe the dynamic markings.

Exercise #10

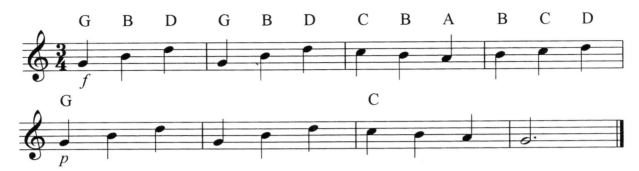

Memorize the following dynamics chart.

Dynamics Chart (always use small cursive letters to show dynamics.)

	Markings for "softs" in music				Markings for "louds" in music		
p	=	*piano*	=	soft	***f***	=	*forte*	=	loud
mp	=	*mezzo piano*	=	moderately soft	***mf***	=	*mezzo forte*	=	moderately loud
pp	=	*pianissimo*	=	very soft	***ff***	=	*fortissimo*	=	very loud

---

LESSON V PIECES

Beautiful Savior

Words by German Jesuits
Trans. by J.A. Seiss (1873)

Crusader hymn / Silesian folk song
Arr. by Lois Veenhoven Guderian

Prelude II

Music by Lois Veenhoven Guderian

Aura Lee

Words by G. R. Poulton

Music by W.W. Fosdick, ca. 1830
Arr. by Lois Veenhoven Guderian

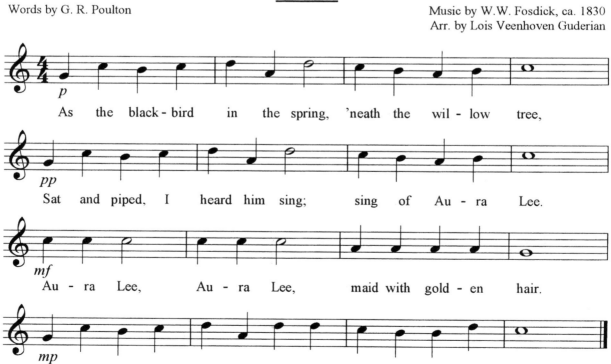

As the black-bird in the spring, 'neath the wil-low tree,

Sat and piped, I heard him sing; sing of Au-ra Lee.

Au-ra Lee, Au-ra Lee, maid with gold-en hair.

Sun-shine came a-long with thee, and swal-lows in the air.

CREATIVE CORNER

Add dynamic markings to one or more of the compositions you have composed.

THEORY AND TERMS FROM LESSON V

Dynamics

p   = *piano*

mp = *mezzo piano*

pp = *pianissimo*

f   = *forte*

mf = *mezzo forte*

ff   = *fortissimo*

ASSIGNMENT

1. Practice Exercise #9.

2. Practice Exercise #10 with the *p* and *f* dynamic markings.

3. Practice **LESSON V PIECES** with dynamics: *Beautiful Savior*, *Prelude II*, and *Aura Lee*.

4. Complete the **CREATIVE CORNER** section.

5. Memorize the **Dynamics Chart**.

6. Keep a chart of your practice time.

M	TU	W	TH	F	SA	SU

TECHNIQUE AND FINGERING

Four New Notes – Middle C, Middle D, Middle E and Middle F

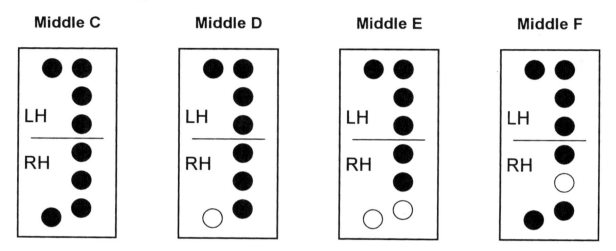

Small hands may eliminate
finger #5 of RH

Practice Exercise #11 to learn the fingerings for middle C, D, E and F. Play it 𝒇 *forte* (loud) the first time and 𝒑 *piano* (soft) the second time.

Exercise #11

MUSIC LESSON

C Major Scale

The C major scale is made up of eight steps. In reading Western music notation from left to right, if the first note of the scale begins on a line, the second note is placed on the very next space. Likewise, when the scale begins on a space, the second note is placed on a line thus creating an "interval" (the distance between two notes) called a "second." This rule applies in both ascending (going up) and descending (going down) directions. Notes written in ascending direction sound higher and higher. Notes written in descending direction sound lower and lower. Example #2 below shows the ascending scale steps in measures 1 & 2; descending scale steps in measures 3 & 4. Seconds (steps) are just one kind of interval.

Example #1: Steps or 2nds

Example #2: The C Major Scale

The scale can be sung on letters, solfège syllables (a traditional system of syllables often used in learning to sing the eight-step major scale: do, re, mi, fa, sol, la, ti, do), numbers, or a syllable of your choice such as "loo," "la," "mi," and so forth.

Sing the scale in each of the above ways using letters, solfège syllables, numbers, and a syllable of your choice.

Play the C major scale on your recorder using the new notes C, D, E, and F for the first half of the scale and the notes G, A, B, and C for the second half of the scale.

Practice Exercise #12, *Come Back Home*, using the new notes you have learned.

The end of a piece usually has a double bar. When the double bar is preceded by two dots it is called a "repeat sign." When a repeat sign is at the end of a piece, go back to the beginning and play it again.

Come Back Home has many skips. Skips are played by "skipping" steps. Study the differences in notation for steps, skips, and repeated notes.

Exercise #12

Come Back Home

LESSON VI PIECES

Burleske

Music by Leopold Mozart
Arr. by Lois Veenhoven Guderian

Holy, Holy, Holy

Words by Reginald Heber

Music by Rev. John B. Dykes
Arr. by Lois Veenhoven Guderian

Ho - ly, Ho - ly, Ho - ly, Lord God Al - might - y!

Ear - ly in the morn - ing our song shall rise to Thee.

Ho - ly, Ho - ly, Ho - ly, Mer - ci - ful and Might - y!

God in Three per - sons, bless - ed Trin - i - ty!

CREATIVE CORNER

Practice *Twinkle, Twinkle Little Star*. Then play the variation of *Twinkle, Twinkle Little Star*.
Try creating your own variation of *Twinkle, Twinkle Little Star* by changing some of the notes,
rhythm, and/or dynamics. A staff is provided for your variation.

Twinkle, Twinkle Little Star

Traditional French tune

Twinkle, Twinkle Little Star
Variation I

Twinkle, Twinkle Little Star
Variation II

THEORY AND TERMS FROM LESSON VI

Step — an interval of a second.

Interval — the distance between two tones.

Skip — an interval larger than a second.

C Major Scale — comprised of eight steps in ascending or descending order, or seconds.

Repeat Sign — directs you to go back to the beginning and play again (when placed at the end of a piece).

Syllable — a vowel, preceded by a consonant, used to exercise the singing voice.

Solfège — a traditional system of syllables used in learning to read music. The solfège syllables are often used in learning to sing the eight-step major scale (do, re, mi, fa, sol, la, ti, do).

ASSIGNMENT

1. Sing the C major scale on letters, numbers, and solfège syllables.

2. Practice playing the C major scale, ascending and descending, on the recorder.

3. Create your own variation of *Twinkle, Twinkle Little Star*.

4. Practice the pieces *Come Back Home; Burleske; Holy, Holy, Holy; Twinkle, Twinkle Little Star;* and your own variation of *Twinkle, Twinkle Little Star*.

5. Learn the **THEORY AND TERMS** from **LESSON VI**.

6. Keep a chart of your practice time.

M	TU	W	TH	F	SA	SU

TECHNIQUE AND FINGERING

Practice playing the C major scale, ascending and descending. Be sure to tongue each note.

MUSIC LESSON

The Pickup

A pickup note or notes (also called "upbeat") precede the first full measure of music.

Example:

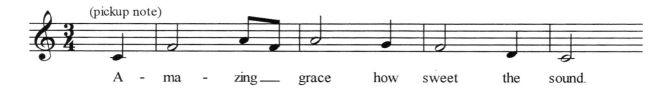

A pickup note or notes (the upbeat) do not receive an accent. The pickup is played softer than the first beat of the first measure (the downbeat). The last measure in the example above has two beats. The third beat of the measure is the pickup at the beginning of the piece.

Clap and count Exercise #13.

Exercise #13

LESSON VII PIECES

Peaceful Evening

Music by Lois Veenhoven Guderian

Amazing Grace

Words by John Newton

Early American tune
Arr. by Lois Veenhoven Guderian

A - maz - ing__ grace, how sweet the sound, That saved a__

wretch like me;_____ I once__ was_ lost but now__ I'm_

found, Was blind, but__ now I see._____

CREATIVE CORNER

Create your own composition in ¾ time using the notes and note values you have learned. Begin your piece with a pickup note. Eight measures have been provided for your piece. Add or subtract measures according to your creative needs.

THEORY AND TERMS FROM LESSON VII

Pickup Note or Notes (Upbeat) — precede the first full measure of music

Downbeat — the first beat of the measure

ASSIGNMENT

1. Clap the rhythm of Exercise #13.

2. Practice playing the pickup example of Exercise #13.

3. Practice the new pieces of **LESSON VII**: *Peaceful Evening* and *Amazing Grace*.

4. Complete the **CREATIVE CORNER** section of **LESSON VII**.

5. Learn the **THEORY AND TERMS** from **LESSON VII**.

6. Keep a chart of your practice time.

M	TU	W	TH	F	SA	SU

LESSON VIII

TECHNIQUE AND FINGERING

Reviewing What You Have Learned

Review all of the fingerings you have learned by practicing Exercise #14, the C major scale plus one note. Practice the exercise three times playing it *piano* the first time, *mezzo forte* the second time, and *forte* the third time.

Exercise #14

Practice playing the skips and steps in Exercise #15, tonguing each note. Remember, correct tonguing can be achieved by saying the "tah" syllable while the recorder is held between the lips. Long held notes can be stopped by making the "d" sound with the tongue.

Exercise #15

MUSIC LESSON

Dotted Quarter Note

Many pieces contain a dotted quarter note. A dot to the side of a note, where the stem and note head meet, gives an additional one half the time value of the note. In 2/4, 3/4, 5/4, 6/4 and 4/4 time, a quarter note is one beat. A dotted quarter note is one and one half beats.

THE DOTTED QUARTER NOTE ———— 𝅘𝅥. ———— **RECEIVES 1½ BEATS**

Clap and count the dotted quarter note, the eighth note, and the steady quarter notes in Exercise #16.

Exercise #16

Clap and count the rhythm pattern in Exercise #17.

Exercise #17

The Dotted Quarter Note in Famous Songs

Step 1. Say the words of the following famous tune excerpts as you clap the rhythm.

Step 2. Count out loud as you clap the rhythm of each famous tune excerpt.

Step 3. Play the famous tune excerpts on your recorder.

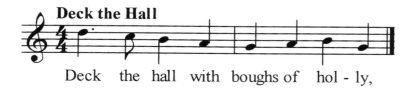

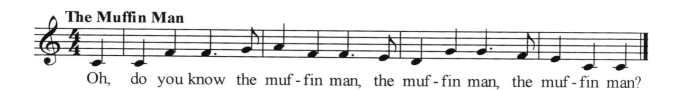

LESSON VIII PIECES

Deck the Hall

Traditional lyrics

Old Welsh tune
Arr. by Lois Veenhoven Guderian

Deck the hall with boughs of hol - ly, Fa la la la la, la la la la.

'Tis the sea - son to be jol - ly, Fa la la la la, la la la la.

Don we now our best ap - par - rel, Fa la la la la la, la la la.

Troll the an - cient Yule - tide car - ol, Fa la la la la, la la la la.

Largo

Music by A. Dvorak (from the *New World Symphony*)
Arr. by Lois Veenhoven Guderian

CREATIVE CORNER

Compose a four measure rhythm composition containing the dotted quarter note and eighth note rhythm pattern. Use one of the following meters: 2/4, 3/4, or 4/4.

Example:

Make copies of your composition and teach it to a friend, family member, your teacher, or your class.

THEORY AND TERMS FROM LESSON VIII

Dotted Quarter Note (♩.) — receives 1½ beats in time signatures where the quarter note receives one beat. (When the notated time signature has a "4" on the bottom.)

ASSIGNMENT

1. Practice the famous tune excerpts. Say the words aloud as you clap the rhythm of each one. Follow this by counting aloud as you clap the rhythm of each, and finally, play the excerpt on your recorder.

2. Practice the **PIECES of LESSON VIII**: *Deck the Hall* and Dvorak's *Largo*. Learn the **THEORY AND TERMS** of **LESSON VIII**.

3. Complete the **CREATIVE CORNER** section of **LESSON VIII**.

4. Keep a chart of your practice time.

M	TU	W	TH	F	SA	SU

LESSON IX

New Note – F Sharp (F♯)

F Sharp

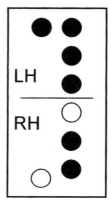

A sharp sign (♯) placed to the left of a note on the staff raises the tone one half step. Another name for a ♯ is an accidental. An accidental either raises or lowers a tone. A "sharped" note has its own fingering. The most commonly sharped note is F sharp.

Find the fingering for F♯ on your recorder. Practice Exercise #18a.

Exercise #18a

Practice Exercise #18b. Can you find the small difference between #18a and #18b? In the second measure of #18b, only the first F is marked as sharp. The rule in writing music is: If a note is marked with a sharp sign, repetitions of that note within the same measure will also be sharped. The second half note in measure #2 of Exercise #18b is still sharped; however, it is not necessary to mark it with a sharp sign.

Exercise #18b

M U S I C   L E S S O N

Key Signature

When a sharp is placed on the F line of the staff at the beginning of the piece, all Fs in the piece are sharped. This is referred to as the "key signature." The key signature also appears at the beginning of each new line. The key signature of Exercise #18c is one sharp. The word *allegro* appears at the beginning of the exercise. *Allegro* (ah-**leh**-groh) is the Italian word for fast and lively. Practice Exercise #18c. Be sure to observe the key signature and be sure to play the exercise fast and lively.

Exercise #18c

Another Italian term is *da capo al fine*. When this term, or abbreviated term *D.C. al fine* appears in the music, it is an indication to go back to the beginning, repeating the music until the word *Fine* occurs in the music. *Da capo al fine* literally means: "Go to the head until you reach the finish." The piece *Reminiscent of an Old Dance* contains a *D.C. al fine*.

LESSON IX PIECES

Nearer My God to Thee

Words by Sarah F. Adams

Music by Lowell Mason
Arr. by Lois Veenhoven Guderian

Reminiscent of an Old Dance

Music by Lois Veenhoven Guderian

CREATIVE CORNER

Play the following piece on your recorder. Should this piece have a *D.C. al fine*? If so, where should the *D.C. al fine* be placed in the music? Write the *D.C. al fine* where you think it should go. Remember to place a double bar where you write the *D.C. al fine* and a final bar marking with the word *Fine* where you think the piece should end. You may want to add other markings as well such as repeat signs and dynamics.

THEORY AND TERMS FROM LESSON IX

Sharp (♯) — raises a tone one half step.

Accidental — raises or lowers a tone one half step.

Key Signature — shows the sharps or flats of a piece.

Allegro — Italian for fast and lively.

D.C. al fine — means go back to the beginning until the *Fine* or finish of the piece.

Double Bar — two bar lines drawn close together to mark the end of a section or piece; usually thicker when placed at the end of a piece.

ASSIGNMENT

1. Study and memorize the **THEORY AND TERMS** from **LESSON IX**.

2. Practice the **PIECES of LESSON IX**: *Nearer My God to Thee* and *Reminiscent of an Old Dance*.

3. Review and practice Exercises #18a, #18b and #18c.

4. Complete the **CREATIVE CORNER** assignment.

5. Keep a chart of your practice time.

M	TU	W	TH	F	SA	SU

LESSON X

New Note – B Flat (B♭)

B Flat

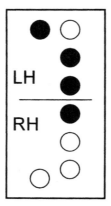

A flat sign (♭) placed to the left of a note on the staff lowers the tone one half step. A flatted note has its own fingering. The most commonly flatted note is B.

Find the fingering for B♭ on your recorder. Practice Exercise #19a. The rule in music is if a note is marked with an accidental, that is, a sharp, flat, or natural sign, repetitions of that note within the same measure will also be sharp, flat or natural. Remember to keep the flat for both Bs in measure #3.

Exercise #19a

Practice Exercise #19b. The key signature of Exercise #19b is one flat. Be sure to observe the key signature by playing all of the Bs flat. Be sure to look for the key signature between the treble clef sign and the time signature before playing a piece.

Exercise #19b

MUSIC LESSON

Terms of Expression and Tempo

Words of expression and tempo are used by composers to indicate how their music should be played. These words appear above the time signature and staff. The word "tempo" refers to the speed of the piece. Often, a metronome marking is included indicating a more precise interpretation of the tempo terms. The metronome normally can be set from 40 to 210 beats per minute. Words of expression and tempo are written in many languages; however, the Italian language is used most often. Italian terms of expression and tempo are learned by musicians all over the world. The following list contains a few of the most commonly used terms.

Tempo terms

Term	Pronunciation	Meaning
Adagio	(ah-**dah**-zshee-oh)	to play or sing a piece in a slow tempo
Allegro	(ah-**leh**-groh)	to play or sing a piece fast and lively
Andante	(ahn-**dahn**-tay)	to play or sing a piece in a moderate walking tempo
Largo	(**lahr**-goh)	to play or sing a piece in a very slow tempo
Moderato	(mah-der-**ah**-toh)	to play or sing a piece in a moderate tempo
Presto	(**pres**-toh)	to play or sing a piece in a fast tempo

Expression words

Term	Pronunciation	Meaning
Cantabile	(cahn-**tah**-bee-leh)	to play or sing a piece in a flowing, singing manner
Espressivo	(es-pres-**see**-voh)	to play or sing a piece expressively
Giocoso	(jee-oh-**koh**-soh)	to play or sing a piece in a lively, joking manner
Grazioso	(grah-tsee-**oh**-soh)	to play or sing a piece gracefully
Maestoso	(mah-eh-**stoh**-soh)	to play or sing a piece in a majestic manner

LESSON X PIECES

Learn the pieces of LESSON X. Be careful to observe the key signature, time signature, and terms of expression and tempo for each piece.

Brother Come and Dance With Me

Music by E. Humperdinck
Arr. by Lois Veenhoven Guderian

Bird Song at Evening

By Lois Veenhoven Guderian

God Be with You Till We Meet Again

Words by J. E. Rankin

Music by W. G. Tomer
Arr. by Lois Veenhoven Guderian

CREATIVE CORNER

Finish the following short melody by creating an "answer" to the first phrase "question." Ending on F or A will keep the example in the key in which it started, the key of F with one flat.

THEORY AND TERMS FROM LESSON X

Flat (♭) — lowers a tone one half step

Tempo Terms

Term	Pronunciation	Meaning
Adagio	(ah-**dah**-zshee-oh)	to play or sing a piece in a slow tempo
Allegro	(ah-**leh**-groh)	to play or sing a piece fast and lively
Andante	(ahn-**dahn**-tay)	to play or sing a piece in a moderate walking tempo
Largo	(**lahr**-goh)	to play or sing a piece in a very slow tempo
Moderato	(mah-der-**ah**-toh)	to play or sing a piece in a moderate tempo
Presto	(**prehs**-toh)	to play or sing a piece in a fast tempo

Expression Words

Term	Pronunciation	Meaning
Cantabile	(cahn-**tah**-bee-lay)	to play or sing a piece in a flowing, singing manner
Espressivo	(es-pres-**see**-voh)	to play or sing a piece expressively
Giocoso	(jee-oh-**koh**-soh)	to play or sing a piece in a lively, joking manner
Grazioso	(grah-tsee-**oh**-soh)	to play or sing a piece gracefully
Maestoso	(my-**stoh**-soh)	to play or sing a piece in a majestic manner

---

ASSIGNMENT

1. Practice Exercises #19a and #19b.

2. Practice the **PIECES of LESSON X**: *Brother Come and Dance with Me, Birdsong at Evening,* and *God Be With You Till We Meet Again*.

3. Learn the **THEORY** and **TERMS** of **LESSON X**.

4. Complete the **CREATIVE CORNER** section.

5. Keep a chart of your practice time.

M	TU	W	TH	F	SA	SU

LESSON XI

TECHNIQUE AND FINGERING

To review and reinforce the fingering for F$\sharp$ and B$\flat$, practice Exercises #20 and #21 three times each.

Exercise #20

Exercise #21

MUSIC LESSON

Rests

Many times, pieces of music contain rests. Rests are beats, or parts of beats, that have no sound. For each note symbol, there is a corresponding rest symbol. Observe the following table of rests.

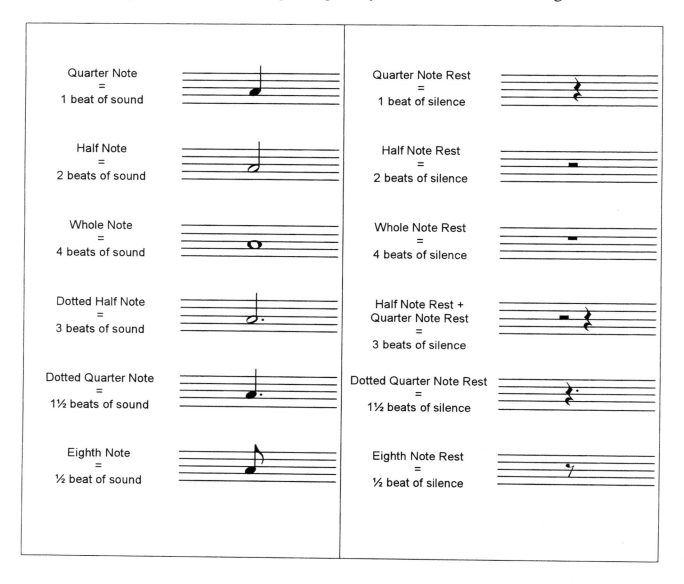

Quarter Note
=
1 beat of sound

Quarter Note Rest
=
1 beat of silence

Half Note
=
2 beats of sound

Half Note Rest
=
2 beats of silence

Whole Note
=
4 beats of sound

Whole Note Rest
=
4 beats of silence

Dotted Half Note
=
3 beats of sound

Half Note Rest +
Quarter Note Rest
=
3 beats of silence

Dotted Quarter Note
=
1½ beats of sound

Dotted Quarter Note Rest
=
1½ beats of silence

Eighth Note
=
½ beat of sound

Eighth Note Rest
=
½ beat of silence

Clap Exercises #22 and #23. Tap the air where there are rests. This will help you to feel the beats. Count aloud as you clap each exercise.

Exercise #22

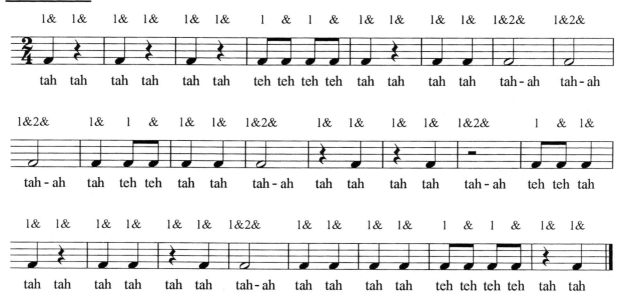

Exercise #23

LESSON XI PIECES

Practice the following pieces. For rests, stop the tone by thinking "d." Be sure to feel a rest for its full value.

Jacob's Ladder

Traditional lyrics

African American Spiritual
Arr. by Lois Veenhoven Guderian

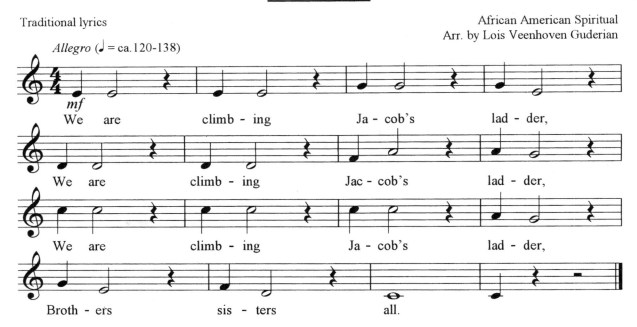

Clap the rhythm of the piece *Playing Statues* before you practice the piece on your recorder.

Playing Statues

Music by Lois Veenhoven Guderian

Before practicing *Joshua Fit the Battle,* clap and count the following syncopated rhythms of Exercies #24a and #24b (same rhythm, two different ways of counting). Syncopated rhythms are lively, snappy rhythms in which the accent of the rhythm does not fall on the usually accented first beat of the measure. Count aloud for precision. Remember to "tap the air" for the rests.

Exercise #24a

Exercise #24b

Joshua Fit the Battle

Traditional lyrics

African American Spiritual
Arr. by Lois Veenhoven Guderian

CREATIVE CORNER

Create your own rhythm composition.

1. Make your composition 4 to 8 measures long.

2. Use 2/4, 3/4, or 4/4 time signature.

3. Be sure to include rests.

4. Compose your piece for one or more instruments.

5. Use traditional or homemade rhythm instruments.

6. Teach your piece to a friend or to your class.

A rhythm composition does not need to be written on staff paper, but may be. Use the staff paper below or create your own system of notating your work.

THEORY AND TERMS FROM LESSON XI

Syncopation — displaces the accent from the usually accented beat. Syncopated rhythms are found in several styles of music and are characteristic of jazz, rock, African American spirituals and South American styles of music.

Table of Rests in Time Signatures Where the Quarter Note is Equal to One Beat

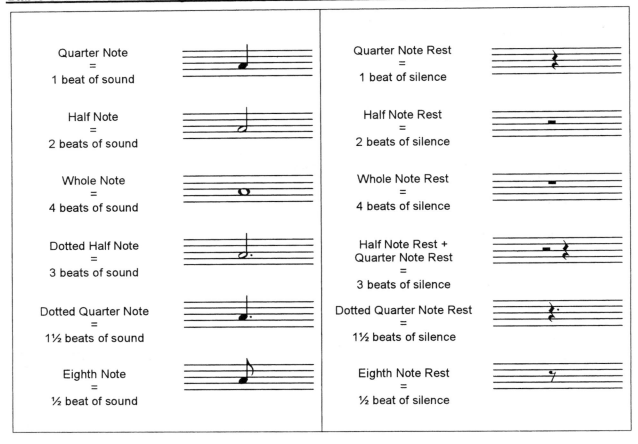

Quarter Note = 1 beat of sound

Half Note = 2 beats of sound

Whole Note = 4 beats of sound

Dotted Half Note = 3 beats of sound

Dotted Quarter Note = 1½ beats of sound

Eighth Note = ½ beat of sound

Quarter Note Rest = 1 beat of silence

Half Note Rest = 2 beats of silence

Whole Note Rest = 4 beats of silence

Half Note Rest + Quarter Note Rest = 3 beats of silence

Dotted Quarter Note Rest = 1½ beats of silence

Eighth Note Rest = ½ beat of silence

ASSIGNMENT

1. Practice playing Exercises #20 and #21.

2. Practice clapping and counting exercises #22, #23, #24a and #24b.

3. Practice the new pieces of **LESSON XI**: *Jacob's Ladder*, *Playing Statues*, and *Joshua Fit the Battle*

4. Complete the **CREATIVE CORNER** section.

5. Memorize the **Table of Rests**.

6. Keep a chart of your practice time.

M	TU	W	TH	F	SA	SU

LESSON XII

TECHNIQUE AND FINGERING

Three New Notes – High E, High F, and High G

The high E, F, and G notes are played by covering only part of the thumb hole of the left hand (about half). The complete fingerings for high E, F and G are shown below. Notice how similar the fingerings are to the lower E, F and G.

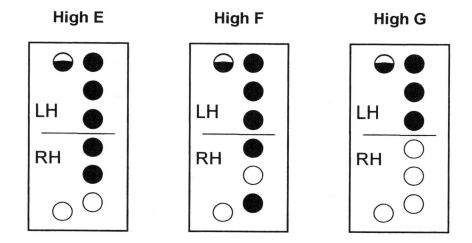

High E, F, and G are notated on the staff in the following way:

Practice playing several high E, F, and G notes. Then, practice Exercise #25 several times to learn to play the notes easily.

Exercise #25

MUSIC LESSON

The Tie

Sometimes, notes of the same pitch are "tied" together to create a longer note value. The tone is held for the sum of the note values tied together. Often, ties occur over a bar line. Study the example below. Play and hold the G counting silently for six beats.

Example:

The curved line connecting the whole note and half note G's is the "tie."

Exercise #26 contains a tie from measure #1 to #2, and a fermata in measure #3. In most music, a **fermata** (fair-**mah**-tah) **sign** placed over a note indicates a holding of the note longer than the normal duration. In **chorales** – hymn tunes from the Baroque time (1600-1750) – a fermata was used to show the end of a line. The piece *Wake, Awake, for Night is Flying* is an example of this practice from the seventeenth and eighteenth centuries.

Play and count Exercise #26. Hold the quarter note that has a fermata a little longer than one beat.

Exercise #26

1   1   1   1   2   1   1   1   1   1   (hold)   1   1   2   3   4

LESSON XII PIECES

Higher and Higher Waltz

Music by Lois Veenhoven Guderian

Blest Be the Tie

Words by John Fawcett

Music by Hans G. Naegeli
Arr. by Lois Veenhoven Guderian

Blest be___ the tie___ that binds_____ Our hearts_ in

Chris - tian love;_____ The fel - low - ship___ of

kin___ dred minds__ Is like___ to that___ a - bove.

Wake, Awake, for Night is Flying

Words by Philipp Nicolai (1599)
Trans. by Catherine Winkworth (1858)

Music by Philipp Nicolai
Arr. by Lois Veenhoven Guderian

Wake, a - wake for night is fly - ing; The watch - men on the

heights are cry - ing: A - wake Je - ru - sa - lem, at last! Mid - night

hears the wel - come voi - ces And at the thril - ling cry re - joi -

ces; Come forth, come forth, the night is past; The Bride - groom comes, a -

wake; Your lamps with glad - ness take; Al - le - lu - ia! And

for his mar - riage feast pre - pare For ye must go and meet Him there.

The Ash Grove

Traditional lyrics

Welsh melody
Arr. by Lois Veenhoven Guderian

CREATIVE CORNER

Create a few "music math" examples in 4/4 time signature. Have your class or friends figure out the answers. Be sure to include a few examples of tied notes.

Examples:

Music Math

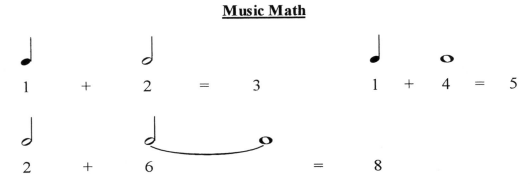

Write your examples here or on a separate sheet.

THEORY AND TERMS FROM LESSON XII

Tie — notes of the same pitch connected by a curved line. Tied notes are held for the sum of the notes tied together.

Fermata — indicates holding a note longer than the normal duration

Chorale — hymn tune from the seventeenth or eighteenth century

---

ASSIGNMENT

1. Practice Exercises #25 and #26 three times each day.

2. Practice the **PIECES of LESSON XII**: *Higher and Higher Waltz; Blest Be the Tie; Wake, Awake for Night is Flying;* and *The Ash Grove*.

3. Complete the **CREATIVE CORNER** section.

4. Learn the **THEORY AND TERMS** of **LESSON XII**.

5. Keep a chart of your practice time.

M	TU	W	TH	F	SA	SU

PLAYING THE SOPRANO RECORDER
A Soprano Recorder Music Method

LESSON XIII

TECHNIQUE AND FINGERING

Practice Exercise #27 at least three times a day. First, learn the exercise at a slow, steady tempo. Increase your speed as you gain facility in playing. No matter what tempo you choose, always work to maintain a steady beat. Facility, or ease in playing, comes from consistent practicing. Playing a piece three or more times per day is practicing.

Exercise #27

MUSIC LESSON

Intervals

An interval is the distance between two tones, or notes. To sing or play from "do" to "re" on the scale is an interval of a second. All steps are intervals of a second. Skips can be thirds, fourths, fifths, etc. Exercise #28 shows the intervals of the C major scale. Practice playing and singing the intervals of Exercise #28 several times. Practicing the intervals will help your eye and musical ear in learning the sight and sound of them.

Exercise #28

Intervals of the C Major Scale

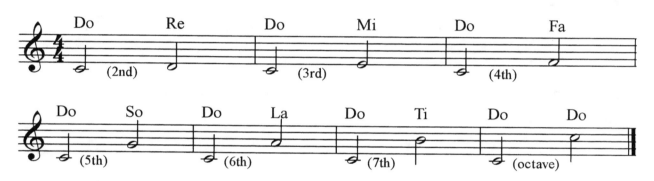

The Natural Sign

A natural sign (♮) placed to the left of a note indicates that the note is neither sharp nor flat. A natural sign is an accidental. The same rules apply for natural signs as for sharps and flats. Study and play the following example.

Example: The Natural Sign

LESSON XIII PIECES

Andante

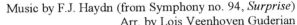

Music by F.J. Haydn (from Symphony no. 94, *Surprise*)
Arr. by Lois Veenhoven Guderian

All Hail the Power of Jesus' Name

(Coronation)

Words by Edward Perronet (1721-1792)

Music by Oliver Holden (1765-1844)
Arr. by Lois Veenhoven Guderian

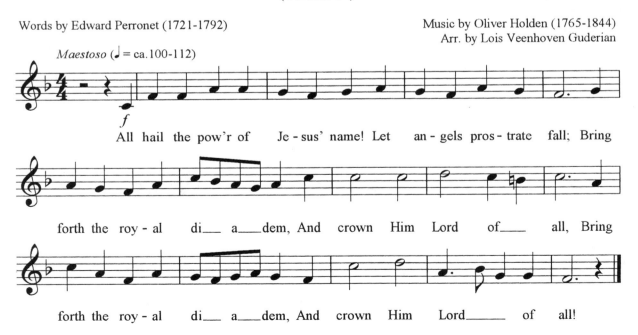

All Through the Night

Words by Sir Harold Boulton (1884)

Traditional Welsh tune
Arr. by Lois Veenhoven Guderian

CREATIVE CORNER

Make a guessing game for your class or friends. Play an interval on your recorder and have your class or friends identify the interval that you played.

THEORY AND TERMS FROM LESSON XIII

Interval — the distance between two tones.

Natural Sign (♮) — indicates that a note is neither sharp nor flat.

ASSIGNMENT

1. Practice Exercises #27and #28.

2. Practice the **PIECES of LESSON XIII**: *Andante* from Haydn's *Surprise* Symphony no. 94 Mov. 2, *All Hail the Power of Jesus' Name,* and *All Through the Night*.

3. Complete the **CREATIVE CORNER** assignment.

4. Memorize the terms.

5. Keep a chart of your practice time.

M	TU	W	TH	F	SA	SU

LESSON XIV

T E C H N I Q U E   A N D   F I N G E R I N G

Accidentals

Practice Exercise #29 to review sharps, flats and naturals.

Exercise #29

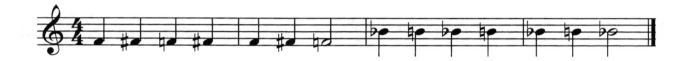

M U S I C   L E S S O N

6/8 Time Signature

In time signatures having the number "**4**" on the bottom of the fraction (4/4, 6/4, 2/4, 3/4, 5/4), the quarter note receives one beat. In 6/8 time signature, the number "**8**" is on the bottom of the fraction. In 6/8 time, the eighth note receives one beat. In all time signatures, the number on the bottom of the fraction indicates the note value that receives the beat.

Read the following aloud:

      4 – There are four beats per measure.
      4 – The quarter note receives one beat.

      2 – There are two beats per measure.
      4 – The quarter note receives one beat.

      3 – There are three beats per measure.
      4 – The quarter note receives one beat.

      6 – There are six beats per measure.
      8 – The eighth note receives one beat.

Note Values in 6/8 Time Signature

The eighth note (♪) receives one beat.

The quarter note (♩) receives two beats.

The dotted quarter note (♩.) receives three beats.

The dotted half note (♩.) receives six beats.

Study and count aloud as you clap Exercise #30.

Exercise #30

In all time signatures, the first beat of the measure receives a "primary," or "strong," accent. In 6/8 time, there is also a "secondary" (less strong) accent on the fourth beat of each measure. This gives the 6/8 meter a feeling of two big beats (count: **ONE** two three **Four** five six) and six small beats per measure. Count aloud while clapping Exercise #31.

Exercise #31

The correct way to count rhythm in 6/8 time is notated underneath the notes in Exercises #30 and #31. In the same manner, notate (write) the correct counting before learning the new pieces of Lesson XIV. Next, count aloud while clapping the rhythm of each piece.

LESSON XIV PIECES

Irish Dance

Music by Lois Veenhoven Guderian

Vivace (♩. = ca.80-92)

Vive la Compagnie

Traditional lyrics

French folk song
Arr. by Lois Veenhoven Guderian

Vivace (♩. = ca.80-96)

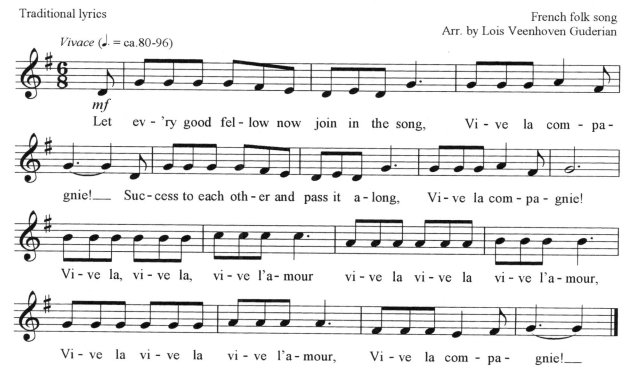

Let ev - 'ry good fel - low now join in the song, Vi - ve la com - pa -

gnie!__ Suc - cess to each oth - er and pass it a - long, Vi - ve la com - pa - gnie!

Vi - ve la, vi - ve la, vi - ve l'a - mour vi - ve la vi - ve la vi - ve l'a - mour,

Vi - ve la vi - ve la vi - ve l'a - mour, Vi - ve la com - pa - gnie!__

Wonderful Words of Life

Music and words by P.P. Bliss
Arr. by Lois Veenhoven Guderian

CREATIVE CORNER

Compose your own melody in 6/8 time. Choose notes from the C major scale. Decide whether or not you want your melody to be stepwise, skipwise, repeated notes or a combination of all of these. Before beginning your composition, practice the C major scale exercise (Exercise #32).

Exercise #32

1 2 3 4 5 6   1 2 3 4 5 6   1 2 3 4 5 6   1 2 3 4 5 6

THEORY AND TERMS FROM LESSON XIV

6/8 Time Signature – means there are six beats per measure. The eighth note receives one beat.

Primary Accent – the first beat of the measure receives emphasis.

Secondary Accent – beat receiving emphasis, however, a slighter emphasis than the first beat of the measure.

Meter – number of beats per measure notated by time signatures. The meter of 4/4 is four beats per measure. The meter of 6/8 is six beats per measure.

ASSIGNMENT

1. Study the **MUSIC LESSON** section. Memorize the list of **Note Values in 6/8 Time Signature**.

2. Practice Exercises #29, #30, #31, and #32.

3. Write in the counting for all the new pieces.

4. Clap the rhythm of the new pieces.

5. Practice the **PIECES of LESSON XIV**: *Irish Dance*, *Vive La Compagnie,* and *Wonderful Words of Life*.

6. Complete the **CREATIVE CORNER** assignment.

7. Keep a chart of your practice time.

M	TU	W	TH	F	SA	SU

PLAYING THE SOPRANO RECORDER
A Soprano Recorder Music Method

LESSON XV

TECHNIQUE AND FINGERING

Staccato Playing

A dot notated above or below a note head indicates staccato playing. Staccato notes are played in a short, crisp, and separated manner. In order to achieve the correct technique for staccato playing, say "taht" for each note as you blow into the recorder. Try the staccato technique as you practice this familiar holiday melody.

Exercise #33 (Piano accompaniment included for this exercise on pp. 72-73 in Section 2.)

Jolly Old Saint Nicholas

Anonymous
Arr. by Lois Veenhoven Guderian

MUSIC LESSON

Sixteenth Note

THE SIXTEENTH NOTE ——— ———— RECEIVES ¼ OF A BEAT

In 4/4 time, the quarter note receives one beat. In a moderate tempo, the quarter note is a "walking" tempo note. The quarter note = one beat. (see Example 1)

Example 1: Quarter Notes

When the quarter note is divided into two parts, eighth notes are created. Eighth notes, often referred to as "running" tempo notes, are faster than quarter notes. Two eighth notes = 1 beat (one eighth note equals ½ of a beat). (See Example 2.)

Example 2: Eighth Notes

When a quarter note is divided into four equal parts, sixteenth notes are created. Sixteenth notes are faster than eighth notes. Sixteenth notes are "fast-running" tempo notes. In 4/4 time, four sixteenth notes = 1 beat (one sixteenth note equals ¼ of a beat). When a piece contains eighth or sixteenth notes, subdivided counting works well to ensure the correct rhythm. There are several ways to count sixteenth notes. Two ways are notated below in Example 3.

Example 3: Sixteenth Notes

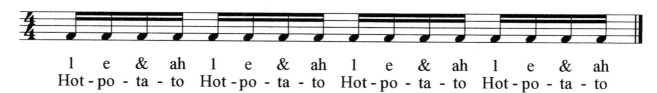

Clap and count Exercise #34. Learn to play Exercise #34 on the recorder. The sixteenth note rest (𝄾) also receives ¼ of a beat in 4/4 time and music where the quarter note is equal to one beat.

Exercise #34

LESSON XV PIECES

The following lively tune, by the nineteenth century songwriter Stephen Foster, contains several interesting sixteenth note rhythm patterns. Count aloud while clapping the rhythm of *Camptown Races* in Exercise #35. Before sight-reading (to play or sing a piece for the first time) the piece on the recorder, sing the song from beginning to end. This will aid in learning the correct rhythm of the piece quickly.

Exercise #35

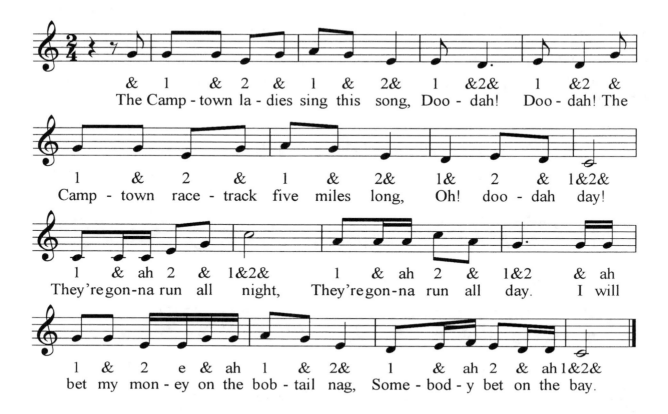

&	1	& 2	& 1	&	2&	1	&2&	1	&2	&

The Camp - town la - dies sing this   song, Doo - dah!   Doo - dah! The

1	&	2	&	1	&	2&	1&	2	&	1&2&

Camp - town race - track five miles long,   Oh! doo - dah   day!

1	& ah	2	&	1&2&	1	& ah	2	&	1&2	& ah

They're gon-na run   all   night,   They're gon-na run   all   day.   I will

1	&	2	e & ah	1	&	2&	1	& ah	2	& ah	1&2&

bet my mon - ey on the bob - tail nag,   Some - bod - y bet on the bay.

Camptown Races

Music and words by Stephen Foster (1826-1864)
Arr. by Lois Veenhoven Guderian

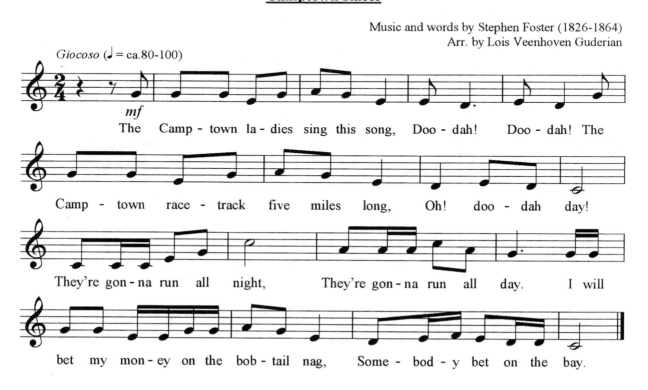

Giocoso (♩ = ca.80-100)

mf

The   Camp - town la - dies sing this song, Doo - dah!   Doo - dah! The

Camp - town race - track   five   miles   long,   Oh!   doo - dah   day!

They're gon - na run   all   night,   They're gon - na run   all   day.   I will

bet   my mon - ey on the bob - tail nag,   Some - bod - y bet on the bay.

Little David Play on Your Harp is another very familiar tune from nineteenth century America. It was created by an African American during slave times. It is a spiritual. As with almost all the beautiful African American spirituals, the composers are anonymous.

Little David Play on Your Harp contains several of the very same rhythm patterns as the piece *Camptown Races*. Clap the rhythm and sing the song before sight reading the piece on your recorder.

Little David Play on Your Harp

Traditional lyrics

African American Spiritual
Arr. by Lois Veenhoven Guderian

Vivace (♩ = ca.88-96)

Lit - tle Da - vid play on your harp, Hal - le - lu, hal - le - lu! Lit - tle Da - vid

play on your harp, hal - le - lu.　Lit - tle Da - vid play on your

harp hal - le - lu, hal - le - lu! Lit - le Da - vid play on your

harp, hal - le - lu.　Lit - tle Da - vid was a

shep - herd boy._____ He killed Go - li - ath and shout-ed for joy.

CREATIVE CORNER

Using the same rhythm of either *Camptown Races* or *Little David Play on Your Harp*, compose a completely new tune. Give your piece a title.

Example: *Camptown Races Revisited*

Use the staff below to write your new melody.

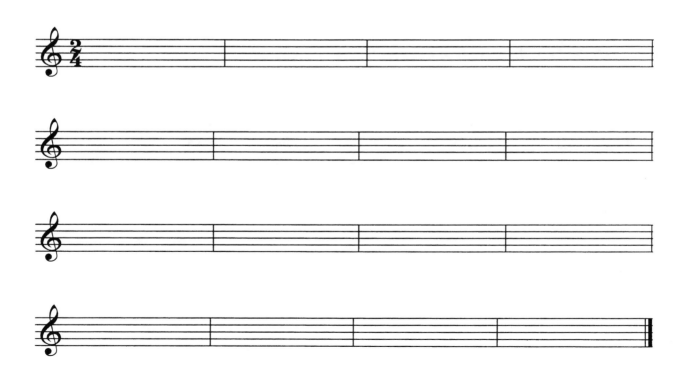

THEORY AND TERMS FROM LESSON XV

Sixteenth Note (♪) – receives ¼ of a beat in 4/4 time.

Sixteenth Note Rest (⅞) – receives ¼ of a beat in 4/4 time.

Sight-reading – to play or sing a piece for the first time.

Subdivide – to divide into smaller parts.

Staccato – to play a note in a short, separated manner. Staccato is notated by placing a dot above or below a note head.

ASSIGNMENT

1. Practice the staccato playing technique in Exercise #33.

2. Practice clapping and counting Exercises #34 and #35.

3. Learn the **PIECES of LESSON XV:** *Camptown Races* and *Little David Play on Your Harp.*

4. Complete the **CREATIVE CORNER** assignment.

5. Learn the **THEORY AND TERMS** from **LESSON XV**.

6. Keep a chart of your practice time.

M	TU	W	TH	F	SA	SU

LESSON XVI

Legato Playing

In music, it is sometimes desirable to play notes in a smooth, connected manner. Legato is the Italian term for smooth, connected playing or singing. Composers notate legato passages by a slur marking in music scores. A slur is a curved line placed under or above the notes. Study the following example.

Example 1

For each note included in the slur, continue the air flow, or breath support, for the tone without tonguing. To end a slur, make a slight "d" sound with your tongue. Practice legato playing and the technique for articulating slurs in Exercise #36.

Exercise #36

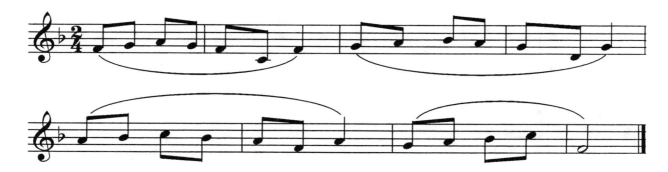

MUSIC LESSON

The Dotted Eighth and Sixteenth Note Rhythm Pattern

A rhythm pattern found in many pieces of music is the dotted eighth and sixteenth note combination. In this pattern, the dotted eighth note receives ¾ of the beat and the sixteenth note receives ¼ of the beat in music where the quarter note is equal to one beat. Study the breakdown of this rhythm pattern below.

Example 2

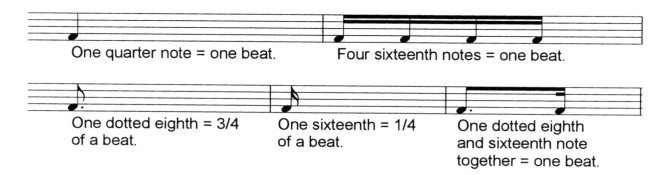

One quarter note = one beat.   Four sixteenth notes = one beat.

One dotted eighth = 3/4 of a beat.   One sixteenth = 1/4 of a beat.   One dotted eighth and sixteenth note together = one beat.

Now clap and play Exercise #37.

Exercise #37

86

LESSON XVI PIECES

Clap and count the rhythm of the piece *Fancy Skip Blues* before playing it on your recorder.

Fancy Skip Blues

Music by Lois Veenhoven Guderian

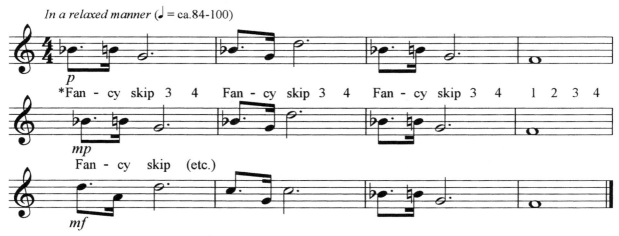

* Speak the words "Fancy Skip" and count aloud to learn the rhythm of *Fancy Skip Blues* more quickly.

Put your new slurring technique to use in the piece *Dream*. Be sure to continue the air flow, or breath support, as you change notes within the slur. *Dream* is written using the C whole-tone scale to suggest a feeling of dreaminess.

Dream

Music by Lois Veenhoven Guderian

The famous song *Battle Hymn of the Republic* contains several dotted eighth and sixteenth note rhythm patterns. Clap the rhythm of the piece while speaking the words notated below Part I.

Learn both Parts I and II of *Battle Hymn of the Republic* on the recorder. Part I is the melody; Part II is a harmony part. Sing the piece, dividing into sopranos on Part I and altos on Part II. Reminder: the fingering for high E requires covering only half of the LH thumb hole.

Battle Hymn of the Republic

Words by Julia Ward Howe

Traditional tune
Arr. by Lois Veenhoven Guderian

CREATIVE CORNER

Learn the following piece on your recorder. After you have played it several times, change the sound by adding slur and staccato markings according to your own musical preference. You will want to experiment with various possibilities before making your final decisions. It is possible that you will create two or three possibilities that you like equally!

THEORY AND TERMS FROM LESSON XVI

Slur – a curved line placed under or above notes of various pitches. A slur indicates legato playing. Slurs can be two or more notes in length. Slurs are played in a smooth, connected manner. The end of a slur is articulated by making a "d" sound with the tongue.

Dotted eighth and sixteenth note rhythm pattern (♪. ♬) – found in meters where the quarter note receives the beat. The pattern is equal to one beat.

Legato – to play in a smooth, connected manner with no tonguing articulation.

ASSIGNMENT

1. Practice Exercise #36 using slurring technique where indicated.

2. Study the dotted eighth and sixteenth note rhythm pattern. Clap, count, and play the rhythm of Exercise #37.

3. Learn the **PIECES** of **LESSON XVI**: *Fancy Skip Blues, Dream,* and *Battle Hymn of the Republic*.

4. Complete the **CREATIVE CORNER** assignment.

5. Learn the **THEORY AND TERMS** from **LESSON XVI**.

6. Keep a chart of your practice time.

M	TU	W	TH	F	SA	SU

LESSON XVII

TECHNIQUE AND FINGERING

To review the fingerings for high E, F, and G, study the Fingering Charts for these notes found on page xxiv and practice Exercise #38. Be sure to slur, tongue, and play staccato where indicated in the music.

Exercise #38

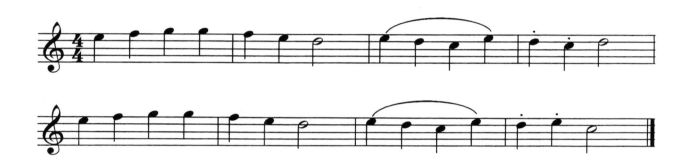

MUSIC LESSON

Eighth and Sixteenth Notes in 6/8 Time

In 6/8 time, sixteenth notes function in the same way eighth notes function in 4/4 time. Study, clap, and count Exercise #39.

Exercise #39

Dotted Eighth Note and Sixteenth Note Patterns in 6/8 Time

In 6/8 time, the dotted eighth and sixteenth note rhythm pattern functions in the same way the dotted quarter and eighth note rhythm pattern functions in 4/4 time. Exercise #40 is the rhythm of the familiar song *Silent Night.* First, clap the rhythm while saying the words. Second, clap and count the rhythm.

Exercise #40

Triplet

A triplet is a group of three notes played in the note value time of two notes of the same kind. When playing or singing a triplet, a little trick to make the triplet rhythmically precise is to count it by using a three syllable word, accent on the first syllable of the word, for each group of triplets. Count aloud while clapping Exercise #41. A triplet is notated in the music with the Arabic number 3 over the three notes that are barred together.

Exercise #41

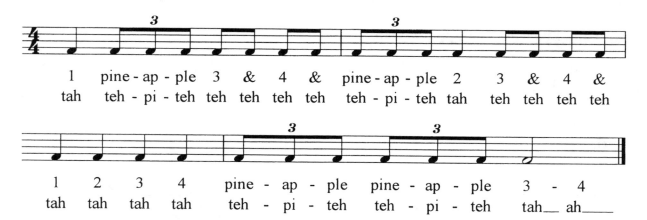

LESSON XVII PIECES

Sur le Pont d'Avignon (On the Bridge of Avignon)

French folk song
Arr. by Lois Veenhoven Guderian

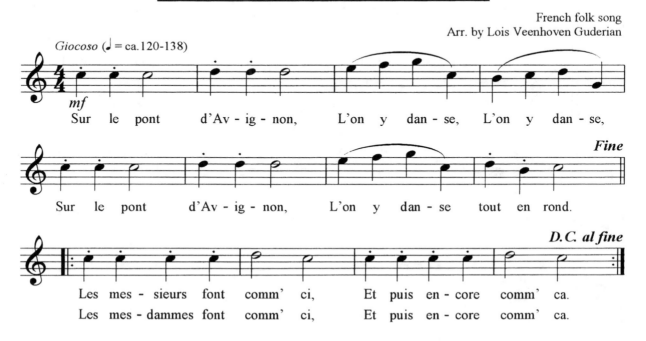

Sur le pont d'Av - ig - non, L'on y dan - se, L'on y dan - se,

Sur le pont d'Av - ig - non, L'on y dan - se tout en rond.

Les mes - sieurs font comm' ci, Et puis en - core comm' ca.
Les mes - dammes font comm' ci, Et puis en - core comm' ca.

Tripleting Along

Music by Lois Veenhoven Guderian

Silent Night / Stille Nacht

Words by Joseph Mohr

Translation from *Carols for Christmastide* (1859) edited by J. Freeman Young

Music by Franz Gruber

Arr. by Lois Veenhoven Guderian

CREATIVE CORNER

Compose an eight-measure rhythm composition in 4/4 time. Use each note value you have learned at least once. Teach a friend, family member, or your class how to play your rhythm composition.

Example:

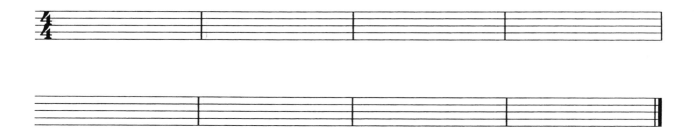

Now write your rhythm composition below.

THEORY AND TERMS FROM LESSON XVII

Triplet – a three-note group played in the note value time of a two-note group. Eighth note triplets (♫♩) are played one group per one beat just as two eighth notes are played one group per one beat.

Dotted eighth and sixteenth note rhythm pattern (♪. ♫) **in 6/8 time** – counted by subdividing the eighth note value.

ASSIGNMENT

1. Practice Exercises #38, #39, #40 and #41.

2. Study the examples of dotted eighth and sixteenth notes in 6/8 time.

3. Study the triplet examples.

4. Complete the **CREATIVE CORNER** assignment.

5. Learn the **THEORY AND TERMS** from **LESSON XVII**.

6. Practice the **PIECES** of **LESSON XVII**: *Sur le Pont D'Avignon*, *Tripleting Along,* and *Silent Night*.

7. Keep a chart of your practice time.

M	TU	W	TH	F	SA	SU

LESSON XVIII

SUPPLEMENTARY SOLOS

Putting it all together

Using what you have learned in this recorder method, learn the pieces that begin on the next page. Be sure to observe every marking in the music.

LESSON XVIII PIECES

Soprano Recorder Part I

Jingle Bells
(Use with or after Lesson I.)

Music by James Pierpont
Arr. by Lois Veenhoven Guderian

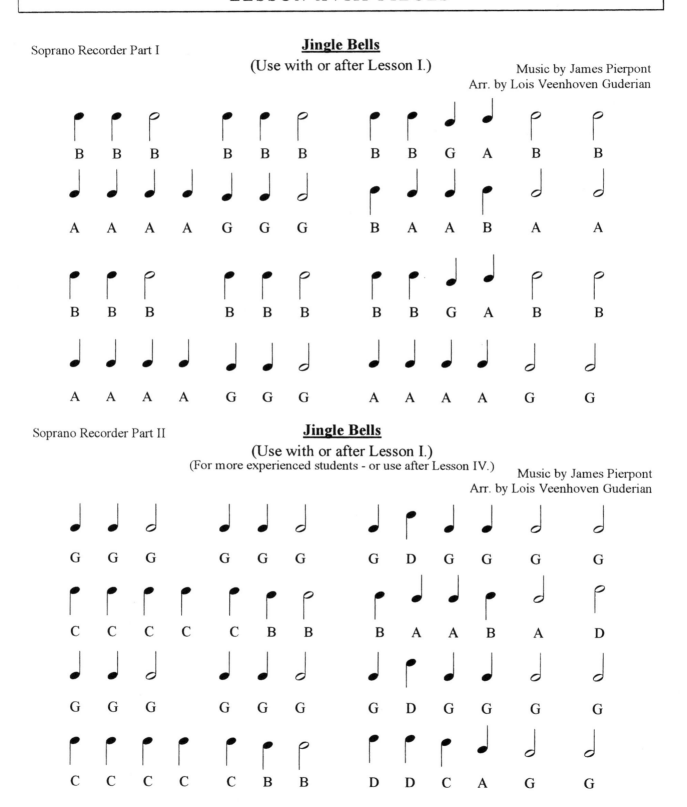

Soprano Recorder Part II

Jingle Bells
(Use with or after Lesson I.)
(For more experienced students - or use after Lesson IV.)

Music by James Pierpont
Arr. by Lois Veenhoven Guderian

Lully, Lullay

(Use with or after Lesson II.)

Anonymous
Arr. by Lois Veenhoven Guderian

God Is Good to Me

(Use Part I with or after Lesson III.)

(Parts II, III and IV are optional and for more experienced students.)   Music and words by
Lois Veenhoven Guderian

<u>Go Tell Aunt Rhodie</u>

(Use with or after Lesson IV.)

Traditional American folk song
Arr. by Lois Veenhoven Guderian

Du Liegst Mir im Herzen

(Use with or after Lesson IV.)

Traditional German folk song
Arr. by Lois Veenhoven Guderian

Stands for three
measures of rest.

Dance for Leila

(Use with or after Lesson V.)

Music by Lois Veenhoven Guderian

Christ the Lord Has Risen Today

(Use Soprano Recorder Part I with or after Lesson VI.)

Words by Charles Wesley (1707-1788)

Anonymous
Arr. by Lois Veenhoven Guderian

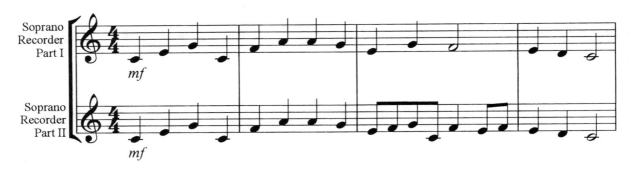

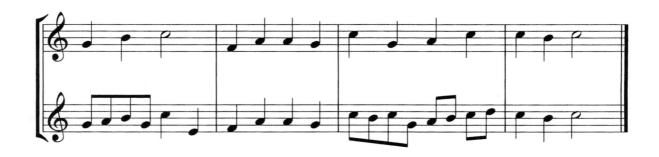

From Heav'n Above to Earth I Come

(Use with or after Lesson VII.)

Music and words by Martin Luther
Arr. by Lois Veenhoven Guderian

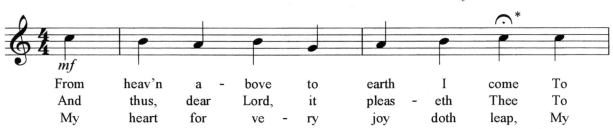

From   heav'n   a - bove   to   earth   I   come   To
And   thus,   dear   Lord,   it   pleas - eth   Thee   To
My   heart   for   ve - ry   joy   doth   leap,   My

bear   good   news   to   ev' - ry   home;   Glad   tid - ings   of   great
make   this   truth   quite   plain   to   me,   That   all   the   world's   wealth,
lips   no   more   can   si - lence   keep;   I,   too,   must   sing   with

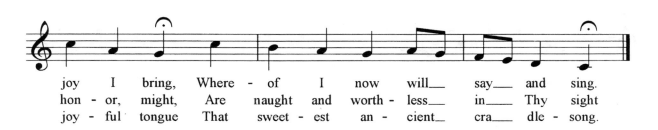

joy   I   bring,   Where - of   I   now   will___   say___   and   sing.
hon - or,   might,   Are   naught   and   worth - less___   in___   Thy   sight
joy - ful   tongue   That   sweet - est   an - cient___   cra___   dle - song.

> * Fermata sign. Hold the note slightly longer than normal.
> See Lesson XII, page 62 for definition of the fermata sign.

Alouette

(Use with or after Lesson VIII.)

Traditional French folk song
Arr. by Lois Veenhoven Guderian

A - lou - et - te,   gen - tille A - lou - et - te,   A - lou - et - te

Je te plu - me - rai.   Je te plu - me - rai la tete,   Je te plu - me - rai la tete,

Et la tete, Et la tete. Oh!_____   A - lou - et - te

gen - tille A - lou - et - te,   A - lou - et - te,   Je te plu - me - rai.

Pomp and Circumstance

(Use with or after Lesson IX.)

Music by Edward Elgar
Arr. by Lois Veenhoven Guderian

My Country 'Tis of Thee / God Save the Queen

(Use with or after Lesson X.)

American words by S. F. Smith (1808-1895)
British words attributed to Henry Carey (1740)

Traditional European tune
Arr. by Lois Veenhoven Guderian

My coun - try 'tis of thee, Sweet land of lib - er - ty,
God save our gra - cious Queen, Long live our no - ble Queen,

Of thee I sing: Land where my fa - thers died, Land of the
God save the Queen! Send her vic - to - ri - ous, Hap - py and

pil - grim's pride, From ev__ 'ry__ moun - tain side Let__ free - dom ring!
glo - ri - ous, Long to__ reign o - ver us; God_ save the Queen!

March of the Toy Soldiers

(Use with or after Lesson XI.)

Music by Victor Herbert
Arr. by Lois Veenhoven Guderian

Hatikvah

(Use with or after Lesson XII.)

Melody by Samuel Cohen
Arr. by Lois Veenhoven Guderian

Ode to Joy

(Use with or after Lesson XII.)

Words by Henry Van Dyke (1852-1933)

Music by L. van Beethoven
(from Symphony no. 9 in D minor)
Arr. by Lois Veenhoven Guderian

Joy - ful, joy - ful we a - dore Thee, God of Glo ry,

Lord of love; Hearts un - fold like flow'rs be - fore Thee, Op' - ning to the

sun a - bove. Melt the clouds of sin and— sad - ness, Drive the— dark of

doubt a - way; Giv - er of im - mor - tal glad - ness,

Fill us with the light of day, the light of day._____

There is a Balm in Gilead

(Use with or after Lesson XIII.)

African American Spiritual
Arr. by Lois Veenhoven Guderian

Barcarolle

(Use with or after Lesson XIV.)

Music by J. Offenbach
Arr. by Lois Veenhoven Guderian

Some Folks Do

(Use with or after Lesson XV.)

Music and words by Stephen Foster (1826-1864)
Arr. by Lois Veenhoven Guderian

mf

Some folks like to sigh,   Some folks do,   some folks do; Some folks wish to   die but

that's not me nor you.   Long live the mer - ry, mer - ry heart that laughs both night and

day,   like the Queen   of   Mirth,   no   mat - ter what some folks   say!

Blessing

(Use with or after Lesson XVI.)

Music and words by Lois Veenhoven Guderian

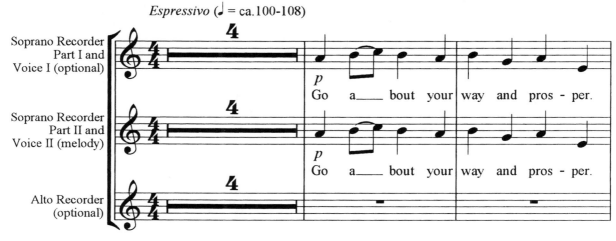

Soprano Recorder Part I and Voice I (optional) / Soprano Recorder Part II and Voice II (melody) / Alto Recorder (optional)

Espressivo (♩ = ca.100-108)

p Go a___ bout your way and pros - per.
p Go a___ bout your way and pros - per.

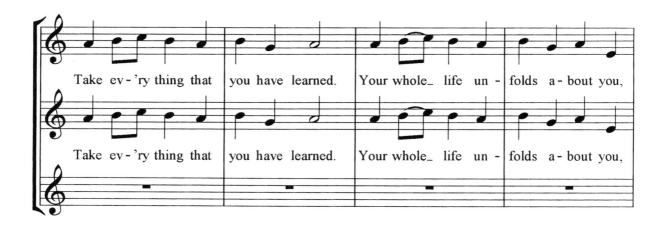

Take ev - 'ry thing that you have learned. Your whole_ life un - folds a - bout you,
Take ev - 'ry thing that you have learned. Your whole_ life un - folds a - bout you,

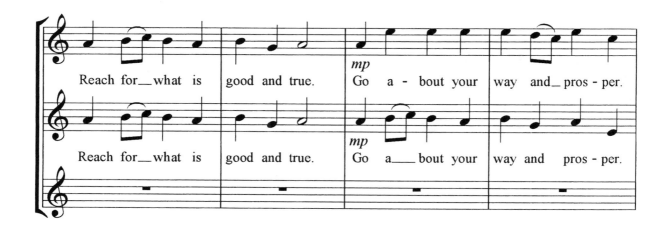

Reach for_ what is good and true. *mp* Go a - bout your way and_ pros - per.
Reach for_ what is good and true. *mp* Go a___ bout your way and pros - per.

Good Christian Men, Rejoice

(Use with or after Lesson XVII.)

Trans. from German by Rev. J.M. Neale

Traditional tune
Arr. by Lois Veenhoven Guderian

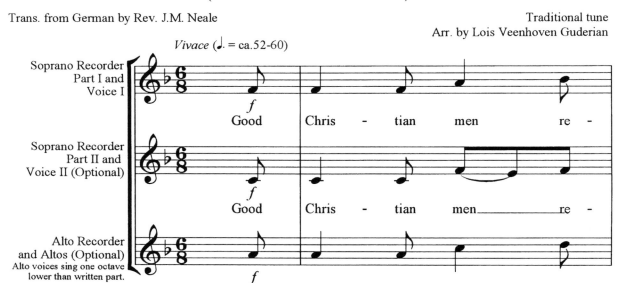

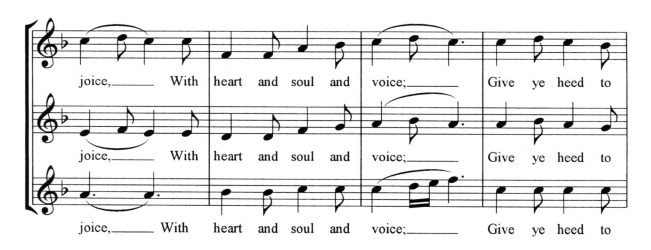

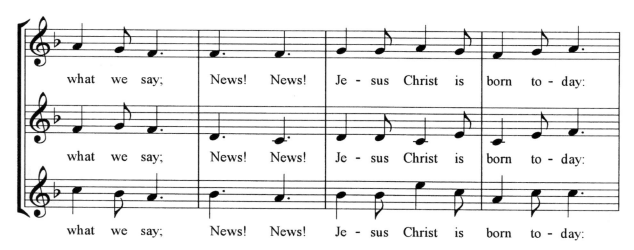

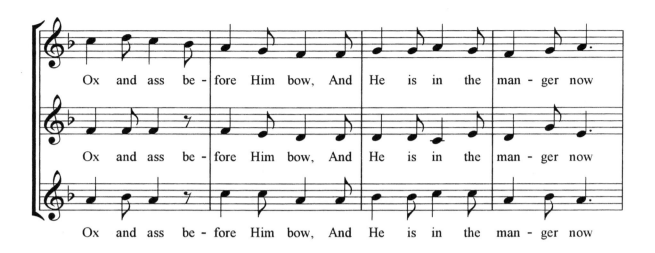

Ox and ass be - fore Him bow, And He is in the man - ger now

Ox and ass be - fore Him bow, And He is in the man - ger now

Ox and ass be - fore Him bow, And He is in the man - ger now

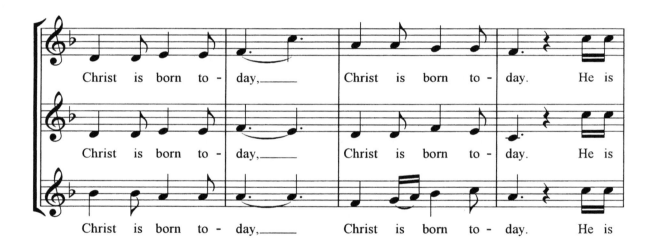

Christ is born to - day,_____ Christ is born to - day. He is

Christ is born to - day,_____ Christ is born to - day. He is

Christ is born to - day,_____ Christ is born to - day. He is

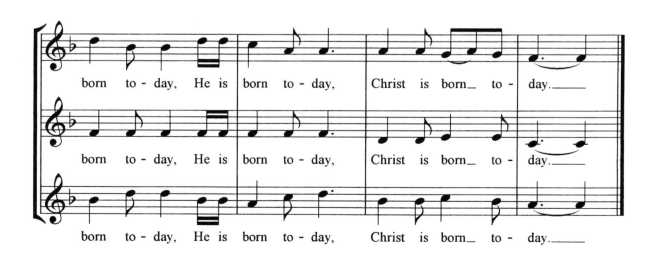

born to - day, He is born to - day, Christ is born__ to - day._____

born to - day, He is born to - day, Christ is born__ to - day._____

born to - day, He is born to - day, Christ is born__ to - day._____

Greensleeves

(Use with or after Lesson XVII.)

Anonymous

Traditional Dorian melody from the Renaissance
Arr. by Lois Veenhoven Guderian

A - las my love_ you do me wrong to cast me off__ dis - cour - teous - ly. For

I have loved__ you oh so long,__ De - light - ing in your com - pa - ny.

Green - sleeves_ was all my joy,__ yes Green - sleeves__ was my de - light.

Green - sleeves was my heart of gold,__ and who but my la - dy Green - sleeves?

MORE SUPPLEMENTARY SOLOS

Abide with Me

Words by Henry Francis Lyte (1793-1847)

Music by William Henry Monk (1823-1889)
Arr. by Lois Veenhoven Guderian

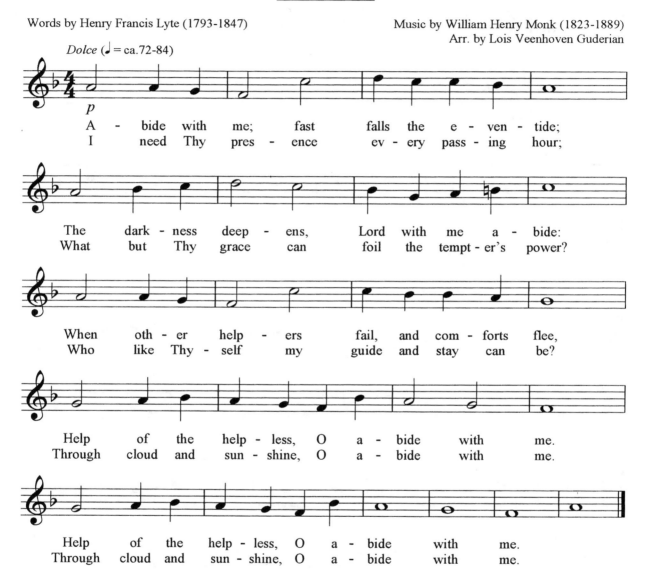

Dolce (♩ = ca.72-84)

p

A - bide with me; fast falls the e - ven - tide;
I need Thy pres - ence ev - ery pass - ing hour;

The dark - ness deep - ens, Lord with me a - bide:
What but Thy grace can foil the tempt - er's power?

When oth - er help - ers fail, and com - forts flee,
Who like Thy - self my guide and stay can be?

Help of the help - less, O a - bide with me.
Through cloud and sun - shine, O a - bide with me.

Help of the help - less, O a - bide with me.
Through cloud and sun - shine, O a - bide with me.

Parson's Farewell

Traditional tune from the Renaissance
Arr. by Lois Veenhoven Guderian

Savior, Like a Shepherd Lead Us

Anonymous

Music by William Bradbury (1816-1868)
Arr. by Lois Veenhoven Guderian

Peacefully (♩ = ca.60-84)

mp

Sav - ior like a shep - herd lead__ us,__ Much we need Thy ten - der care;

In Thy pleas ant pas - tures feed_ us,__ For our use Thy folds pre - pare. Bless - ed

mf

Je - sus, Bless - ed Je - sus, Thou hast bought us, Thine we are; Bless - ed

Je - sus, Bless-ed Je - sus, Thou hast bought us, Thine we are. Bless ed are.

Swing Low, Sweet Chariot / Nobody Knows the Trouble I've Seen

Traditional lyrics

African American Spirituals
Arr. by Lois Veenhoven Guderian

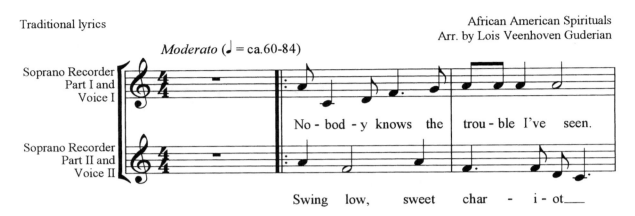

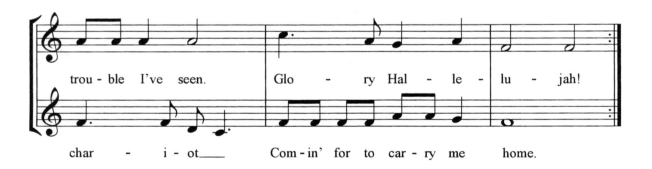

When Peace with the Father Attends My Way

Adapted from lyrics by H.G. Spafford

Music by P.P. Bliss
Arr. by Lois Veenhoven Guderian

Playing the
Soprano
Recorder

Addendum

Glossary

accidental		Raises or lowers a tone one half step.
adagio		To play or sing a piece in a slow tempo.
allegro		To play or sing a piece fast and lively.
andante		To play or sing a piece in a moderate walking tempo.
bar line		Separates the measures.
C major scale		The C major scale is comprised of eight steps, or seconds.
cantabile		To play or sing a piece in a flowing, singing manner.
chorale		A hymn tune from the seventeenth or eighteenth century.
D.C. al fine		Go back to the beginning until the *fine* – finish or end of the piece.
dotted eighth and sixteenth note rhythm pattern		This common rhythm pattern is found in meters where the quarter note receives the beat. The pattern is equal to one beat.
dotted eighth and sixteenth note rhythm pattern in 6/8 time		Count this rhythm by subdividing the eighth note value. In 6/8 meter, the eighth note receives one beat.
dotted half note		Receives three beats in meters where the quarter note receives the beat, i.e. the time signature has a "4" on the bottom.
dotted quarter note		Receives 1½ beats in meters where the quarter note receives the beat, i.e., the time signature has a "4" on the bottom.
double bar		Two measure bar lines drawn close together to mark the end of a section.
double bar, final		Placed at the end of a piece of music.
downbeat		Occurs on the first beat of the measure.
dynamics		The louds and softs of music.
eighth note		Receives ½ beat in meters where the quarter note receives the beat, i.e. the time signature has a "4" on the bottom.
espressivo		To play or sing a piece expressively.

fermata	⌢	A sign that indicates holding a note longer than the normal duration.
flat	♭	A flat sign lowers a tone one half step.
forte	*f*	Loud (a dynamic).
fortissimo	*ff*	Very loud (a dynamic).
giocoso		To play or sing a piece in a lively, joking manner.
grazioso		To play or sing a piece gracefully.
half note	♩	Receives two beats in meters where the quarter note receives the beat, i.e, the time signature has a "4" on the bottom.
interval		An interval is the distance between two tones.
key signature		The sharps or flats at the beginning of a piece that signify the key in which a piece in written.
largo		To play or sing a piece in a very slow tempo.
legato		To play in a smooth, connected manner with no tonguing articulation.
maestoso		To play or sing a piece in a majestic manner.
measure		The space between two measure bar lines.
measure bar line		Separates the measures (same as bar line).
meter		The pattern number of beats per measure notated by time signatures. The meter of 4/4 is four beats per measure. The meter of 6/8 is six beats per measure.
music staff		Five lines and four spaces. Music notes are written on the staff.
mezzo forte	*mf*	Moderately loud (a dynamic).
mezzo piano	*mp*	Moderately soft (a dynamic).
moderato		To play or sing a piece in a moderate tempo.
natural	♮	A natural sign indicates that a note is neither sharp nor flat.
notation (notating, to notate)		The writing of music. Notes on the staff indicate pitch. Note values indicate duration.

notes, tip for writing correctly		Notes placed on the middle line of a staff or higher have stems that go down, on the left side of the note head. Notes placed below the middle line have stems that go up, on the right side of the note head. On the treble staff, G and A are <u>up</u> stem notes. B is a <u>down</u> stem note because it is on the middle line.
pianissimo	***pp***	Very soft (a dynamic).
piano	***p***	Soft (a dynamic).
pickup note or notes (upbeat)		Precede the first full measure of music.
presto		To play or sing a piece in a fast tempo.
primary accent		A strong emphasis: Usually the first beat of the measure receives a strong emphasis or primary accent.
quarter note	♩	Receives one beat in meters where the quarter note receives the beat, i.e., the time signature has a "4" on the bottom.
repeat sign	:‖	Indication to play a section again.
repeated notes		Notes on the same line or space in succession.
rhythm		The result of organizing beats and note values in time.
secondary accent		A beat receiving emphasis, however a slighter emphasis than the first beat of the measure.
sharp	♯	A sharp sign raises a tone one half step.
sight-reading		To play or sing a piece for the first time.
sixteenth note	♬	A sixteenth note receives ¼ of a beat in meters where the quarter note receives the beat, i.e., the time signature has a "4" on the bottom.
sixteenth note rest	♯	A sixteenth note rest receives ¼ of a beat in meters where the quarter note receives the beat, i.e., the time signature has a "4" on the bottom.
skip		Any distance between two notes that is larger than a step, e.g., a line note to the next line note.
slur	‿ or ⌢	A slur is a curved line placed under or above notes of various pitches. A slur indicates legato playing. Slurs can be two or more notes in length. Slurs are played in a smooth, connected manner. The end of a slur is articulated by making a "d" sound with the tongue.

solfège	A traditional system of syllables used in learning to read music. The solfege syllables are often used in learning to sing the eight-step major scale. (do, re, mi, fa, sol, la, ti, do)
staccato	To play a note in a short, separated manner. Staccato is notated by placing a dot above or below a note head.
step	A space note followed by the very next line note, or a line note followed by the very next space note. A step is an interval of a second.
subdivide	To divide into smaller parts.
syllable	A vowel, preceded by a consonant, used to exercise the singing voice.
tie	Tied notes are notes of the same pitch connected by a curved line. Tied notes are held for the sum of the notes tied together.
time signature	Determines the grouping of beats into measures.
treble clef	Also called G clef. Establishes the second line of the staff as G, and is used in notating notes higher in pitch than Middle C.
triplet	A triplet is a three-note group played in the note value time of a two-note group. Eighth note triplets are played one group per one beat just as two eighth notes are played one pair per one beat.
two eighth notes	Equal to one beat in meters where the quarter note receives one beat, i.e., the time signature has a "4" on the bottom.
whole note	Receives four beats in meters where the quarter note receives one beat, i.e., the time signature has a "4" on the bottom.

Tables

Table of Notes and Rests in Time Signatures Where the Quarter Note is Equal to One Beat

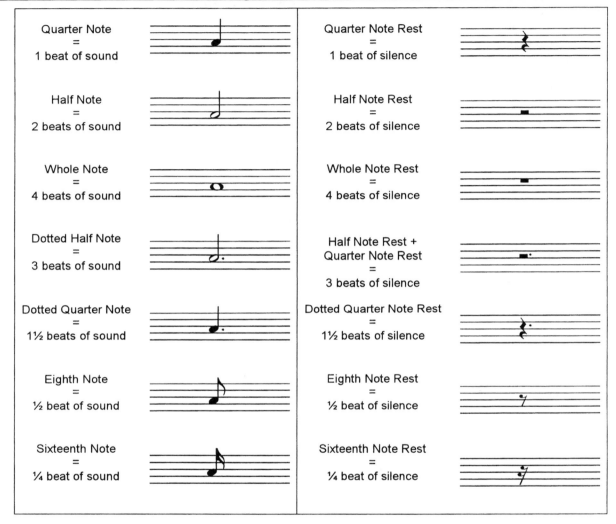

Name of Piece	Lesson	Skills Level same as lesson unless shown	Page Number Lesson	(Complete Edition) Piano Accompaniment
Abide with Me	MSS	XVIII	121	136
All Hail the Power of Jesus' Name	XIII	XIII	70	63
All Through the Night	XIII	XIII	71	64
Andante (Haydn)	XIII	XIII	70	62
Almost a French Folk Song	III	III	16	10
Alouette	XVIII	VIII	106	101
Amazing Grace	VII	VII	35	30
Aura Lee	V	V	26	23
Barcarolle	XVIII	XIV	113	118
Battle Hymn of the Republic	XVI	XVI	88	81
Beautiful Savior	V	V	25	19
Bird Song at Evening	X	X	50	43
Blessing	XVIII	XVI	115	123
Blest Be the Tie	XII	XII	63	56
Breathe on Me Breath of God	II	II	11	6
Brother Come and Dance with Me	X	X	50	42
Burleske	VI	VI	30	25
Camptown Races	XV	XV	81	74
Chester	IV	IV	21	15
Christ the Lord Has Risen Today	XVIII	VI	104	98
Dance for Leila	XVIII	V	103	96
Deck the Hall	VIII	VIII	40	32
Dream	XVI	XVI	87	79
Du Liegst Mir im Herzen	XVIII	IV	102	94
Faith of Our Fathers	II	II	12	7
Fancy Skip Blues	XVI	XVI	87	78
First Piece	I	I	4	1
From Brahms' First	IV	IV	21	17
From Heav'n Above to Earth I Come	XVIII	VII	105	100
Go Tell Aunt Rhodie	XVIII	IV	101	92
God Be with You Till We Meet Again	X	X	51	45
God Is Good to Me	XVIII	III	100	90
God Save the Queen	XVIII	X	108	106
Good Christian Men, Rejoice	XVIII	XVII	118	131
Greensleeves	XVIII	XVII	120	134
Hatikvah	XVIII	XII	110	110
Higher and Higher Waltz	XII	XII	63	55
Holy, Holy, Holy	VI	VI	31	27
Hot Air Balloon Waltz	III	III	17	12

F

Name of Piece	Lesson	Skills Level	Page Number	
		same as lesson unless shown	Lesson	(Complete Edition) Piano Accompaniment
Irish Dance	XIV	XIV	75	66
Jacob's Ladder	XI	XI	56	49
Jingle Bells	XVIII	I	98	87
Jolly Old Saint Nicholas (Exercise #33)	XV	XV	78	72
Joshua Fit the Battle	XI	XI	58	52
Largo (Dvorak)	VIII	VIII	41	34
Little Bird	IV	IV	20	13
Little David Play on Your Harp	XV	XV	82	76
Lully, Lullay	XVIII	II	99	89
March of the Toy Soldiers	XVIII	XI	109	107
My Country 'Tis of Thee / God Save the Queen	XVIII	X	108	106
Nearer My God to Thee	IX	IX	45	37
Nobody Knows the Trouble I've Seen	MSS	XVIII	124	142
Now The Day Is Over	I	I	4	2
Ode to Joy	XVIII	XII	111	112
Parson's Farewell	MSS	XVIII	122	138
Peaceful Evening	VII	VII	35	29
Piece	III	III	16	9
Playing Statues	XI	XI	56	51
Pomp and Circumstance	XVIII	IX	107	103
Praise God from Whom All Blessing Flow	III	III	16	11
Prelude I	I	I	5	3
Prelude II	V	V	26	21
Reminiscent of an Old Dance	IX	IX	46	40
Savior, Like a Shepherd Lead Us	MSS	XVIII	123	140
Silent Night	XVII	XVII	94	85
Some Folks Do	XVIII	XV	114	121
Stop and Look	II	II	10	4
Sur le Pont d'Avignon	XVII	XVII	93	83
Swing Low, Sweet Chariot	MSS	XVIII	124	142
The Ash Grove	XII	XII	65	59
There Is a Balm in Gilead	XVIII	XIII	112	115
Tripleting Along	XVII	XVII	93	84
Twenty-First-Century Minuet	IV	IV	21	18
Vive la Compagnie	XIV	XIV	75	68
Wake, Awake, for Night Is Flying	XII	XII	64	57
Waltz	II	II	11	5
When Peace with the Father Attends My Way	MSS	XVIII	125	145
Wonderful Words of Life	XIV	XIV	76	70

Each piece begins with a short introduction, usually two measures in length.

Track	Title	Time	Track	Title	Time
1	First Piece	00:38	41	Vive la Compagnie	00:33
2	Now the Day Is Over	00:41	42	Wonderful Words of Life	00:54
3	Prelude I	00:36	43	Jolly Old Saint Nicholas (Exercise #33)	00:29
4	Stop and Look	00:23	44	Camptown Races	00:34
5	Waltz	00:35	45	Little David Play on Your Harp	01:05
6	Breathe on Me Breath of God	00:48	46	Fancy Skip Blues	00:46
7	Faith of Our Fathers	00:57	47	Dream	01:47
8	Piece	00:27	48	Battle Hymn of the Republic	01:12
9	Almost a French Folk Song	00:32	49	Sur le Pont d'Avignon	01:01
10	Praise God from Whom All Blessings Flow	00:38	50	Tripleting Along	00:51
11	Hot Air Balloon Waltz	00:41	51	Silent Night	01:05
12	Little Bird	00:39	52	Jingle Bells	00:49
13	Chester	00:56	53	Lully, Lullay	00:57
14	From Brahms' First	00:30	54	God Is Good to Me	00:47
15	Twenty-First-Century Minuet	00:35	55	Go Tell Aunt Rhodie	00:44
16	Beautiful Savior	01:00	56	Du Liegst Mir im Herzen	00:49
17	Prelude II	00:48	57	Dance for Leila	00:46
18	Aura Lee	01:02	58	Christ the Lord Is Risen Today	00:50
19	Burleske	01:16	59	From Heav'n Above to Earth I Come	00:43
20	Holy, Holy, Holy	00:54	60	Alouette	00:35
21	Peaceful Evening	00:35	61	Pomp and Circumstance	01:16
22	Amazing Grace	00:57	62	My Country 'Tis of Thee / God Save the Queen	00:37
23	Deck the Hall	00:46	63	March of the Toy Soldiers	01:34
24	Largo (Dvorak)	01:21	64	Hatikvah	01:14
25	Nearer My God to Thee	01:35	65	Ode to Joy	00:52
26	Reminiscent of an Old Dance	00:43	66	There Is a Balm in Gilead	01:46
27	Brother Come and Dance with Me	01:15	67	Barcarolle	02:50
28	Bird Song at Evening	00:39	68	Some Folks Do	00:33
29	God Be with You Till We Meet Again	01:50	69	Blessing	02:18
30	Jacob's Ladder	00:39	70	Good Christian Men, Rejoice	00:55
31	Playing Statues	00:39	71	Greensleeves	00:56
32	Joshua Fit the Battle	01:18	72	Abide with Me	01:18
33	Higher and Higher Waltz	00:35	73	Parson's Farewell	00:44
34	Blest Be the Tie	00:37	74	Savior, Like a Shepherd Lead Us	01:43
35	Wake, Awake, for Night Is Flying	01:21	75	Swing Low, Sweet Chariot	01:15
36	The Ash Grove	01:32	76	When Peace with the Father Attends My Way	01:44
37	Andante (Haydn)	00:35			
38	All Hail the Power of Jesus' Name	00:44			
39	All Through the Night	01:13			
40	Irish Dance	00:45			